VOLUME ONE

Who DO YOU THINK? You Are!

21 DAY DEVOTIONAL

RAY LEIGHT

Who Do You Think You Are? Volume One: 21 Day Devotional
Copyright © 2016 by Raymond Leight

Requests for information should be addressed to: info@obedienceofbelief.org

Cover Design: Robert Schwendenmann (bobbyhere@gmail.com)
Cover Art: Kyle Williams (kylewilliamsart.org)
Interior Layout and Formatting: Robert Schwendenmann
Editors: Ashley Read (ashleybread@gmail.com) and Melissa Amato (melissa.amato.edits@gmail.com)

ISBN-10: 0-9966989-1-4
ISBN-13: 978-0-9966989-1-7

Please note that the author's publishing style capitalizes certain pronouns in Scripture that refer to Father, Son, Holy Spirit and may differ from other publishers' styles.

VOLUME ONE
21 DAY DEVOTIONAL

This is the 21 Day Devotional for Volume One of 'Who Do You Think You Are?' Both Volumes One and Two are part of the Obedience of Belief™ series. In Volume One, we will explore the truth of our redeemed, alive, righteous, fruitful, pure, and accepted identity in Christ. In Volume Two, we will explore the truth of our loved, known, trusted, pleasing, powerful, and purposeful identity in Christ.

TABLE OF CONTENTS

DEDICATION

Sometimes when I think of the goodness of God and all that Jesus has done for me and my family, I get overwhelmed and can do nothing but cry. I am talking about that ugly kind of cry that would be embarrassing if I wasn't so immersed in His presence.

I get a very similar feeling when I think about my wife, Kathryn, and our two children, Rachel and Riley.

This is dedicated to my family in all of the fullness and love of Jesus!

ACKNOWLEDGEMENTS

There are so many names and faces running through my mind as I think about whom to thank and acknowledge for this devotional. I pray that you all receive the fullness of the immeasurable riches of His grace and kindness in Christ Jesus. I am truly grateful for you.

NOTE FROM THE AUTHOR

Welcome to Volume One of the 'Who Do You Think You Are?' Devotional!

This devotional is intended to complement Volume One of the 'Who Do You Think You Are?' Bible study.

If you haven't had the opportunity to experience the study, this will still be a life-changing process for you. Thank you for your interest in this devotional. I pray that you will experience all the truth, freedom, revelation, and inspiration that the Lord has for you.

HOW TO EXPERIENCE THIS DEVOTIONAL

Each daily segment of this devotional includes several sections to help you know, understand, and believe different aspects of your identity in Christ. With this understanding and faith, you will then be able to establish practical steps toward experiencing these truths in your life.

Here are examples of the different sections and how to experience them:

Question and Expression

Every day will start with a question about your identity.

It is recommended that you start with a time of prayer and then read the question and the corresponding expression of truth. This is intended to get you thinking about what you may already believe about the topic.

After the 'Question and Expression,' there will be Scripture verses that correspond to the question and the expression of truth.

Scripture

Read through the Scriptures and allow the Holy Spirit to reveal what He wants you to know. Take your time and meditate on the truths that God is revealing in His Word.

Here is an example:

For through the law I died to the law, so that I might live to God. I have been crucified with Christ. It is no longer I who live, but Christ who lives in me. And the life I now live in the flesh I live by faith in the Son of God, who loved me and gave Himself for me. I do not nullify the grace of God, for if righteousness were through the law, then Christ died for no purpose. – *Galatians 2:19-21*

Truth and Lies

After the Scripture, you will have an opportunity to process what God is revealing about your identity.

Take a moment to pray and invite God to meet with you as you reflect on the previous verses, and ask the Holy Spirit to reveal the truth of what God is saying in these Scriptures.

Then you will list the truth that was revealed to you:

I have died to the law so that I can live to God.

I have been crucified with Christ.

Christ lives in me, loves me, and gave His life for me.

It is that easy—just list the truth that is revealed to you.

Next you will review the verses one more time, and ask the Lord to reveal any of your thoughts or feelings that may be opposed to these Scriptures.

The reality is, all of us struggle to believe the truth at some level. Anything we believe that is not in alignment with the truth of God's Word is a lie. Let the Lord reveal to you the things you may believe that do not line up with His Word. You are not being tested; this is for your own personal growth. Be honest, and let the Lord reveal these beliefs to you.

List the lies that were revealed:

My sins are too much, and I am bound by the law.

I am still just the same old person I have always been.

I am not loved.

Forgiveness

Then you will review this list and ask the Lord if there is anyone you need to forgive that may have taught you these lies or hurt you with these lies. Keep in mind that forgiveness is not about accusation. We forgive in the same way that the Lord forgave us, by His blood that was shed on the cross (Colossians 3:13). Forgiveness is releasing through the blood of Jesus by the power of the Holy Spirit. That is the only way to forgive. You do not need to understand why someone did what they did, nor do you need to stir up compassion about their own issues first.

As the Lord leads, you will have the opportunity to express forgiveness out loud. There is power in the spoken word (Genesis 1:3; John 15:3).

There will be an example for you to follow:

"In Jesus' name, I choose to forgive _____ for 'teaching me' or 'hurting me with' the lie that _____."

This is just an example—feel free to add anything you wish.

Repentance

You will also have the opportunity to express repentance. A simple definition of repentance is to change your mind. The Word tells us to be transformed by the renewal of our minds (Romans 12:2). Repentance leads to the knowledge of truth and will help us come to our senses and escape from the snare of the enemy (2 Timothy 2:25-26).

You will have the opportunity to repent by breaking agreement with and renouncing the lies you believe. You will also have the opportunity to come into agreement with the truth that the Lord leads you to, thus escaping from any snare of the enemy.

Once you have forgiven, you will have the opportunity to deal with the lies themselves. Since God revealed to you that these are lies, it is time to break agreement with them, renounce them, and forgive yourself for believing them.

Remember, there is power in the spoken word. These are meant to be expressed out loud.

There will be an example for you to follow:

"In Jesus' name, I break agreement and renounce the lie that _____."

"Jesus, I come into agreement with Your forgiveness, and I completely forgive myself for any way I believed those lies. I release all those lies to You."

Statement of Faith

Next, there will be a 'Statement of Faith' available for you to review.

These statements will be a concentration of the verses you have reviewed each day. They are meant for you to read out loud and reflect upon, and let God's truth and love pour into your heart through the Holy Spirit. This can be a very powerful time for you to come into agreement with Jesus and declare His truth over your life (2 Corinthians 4:13).

Now that you have read the verses, reviewed the truth revealed in them, forgiven, and renounced the lies, you will have the opportunity to review the Statement of Faith, and ask God: "What truths about my identity, according to these Scriptures, do You want me to know?"

Jesus really does love me. He lives in me and I am not who I used to be. I truly live when I live by faith in Jesus. I am righteous because Jesus lives in me, not by following the law.

Let yourself dream, and ask God: "How could believing these truths affect my life?"

Feeling loved and knowing that Jesus lives in me, I would be free to be happy, accepted, and capable to do what He created me to do. I wouldn't be limited by fear.

Then you can ask God: "What are some practical steps I can take to experience these truths in my life?"

I can start focusing on what I am really thinking and what I put my faith in. I can reject thoughts of my old self and remind myself of who I am now in Christ.

It is that simple. Just let the Word of God speak to you through the Holy Spirit, and then write that down. Next, let yourself think about how that would affect your life, your relationships, your career, your family, your community, your thinking, etc. Write down whatever God reveals to you. After considering the truth and the effects, you can let God reveal practical steps that you can take to live a life in agreement with these. All of this is for your own personal growth. Let yourself think, dream, and express your heart. You are not being tested; there is no wrong way to do this.

At the end of this process, you will have an opportunity to ask the Holy Spirit to empower these truths and make them more real in your life.

Then, at the end of every day, there will be a list of some of the different aspects of your identity that have been expressed in the Scriptures.

Identity

Take a moment to pray and reflect on these God-given aspects of your identity.

Living to God	Christ in me	Loved
Crucified with Christ	Living by faith	Righteous

Write down a statement of faith of your own:

By the grace of God, I have been crucified with Christ and He lives in me. I am loved, righteous, and I live to God.

May you receive a greater understanding and acceptance of your identity in Christ and be blessed in all the fullness and richness of God's mercy.

Thank you for taking the time to invest in yourself and the world through this devotional.

Be blessed!

Day 1

Are You Redeemed?

*T*hrough the blood of Christ, by the power of the Holy Spirit, we have been released from any curse, penalty, bondage, transgressions, trespasses, or imprisonment. Jesus paid the ransom for our sins with His own blood, thus securing for us an eternal redemption, releasing us as if the sins were never committed.

In Him we have redemption through His blood, the forgiveness of our trespasses, according to the riches of His grace, which He lavished upon us, in all wisdom and insight making known to us the mystery of His will, according to His purpose, which He set forth in Christ as a plan for the fullness of time, to unite all things in Him, things in heaven and things on earth. *– Ephesians 1:7-10*

Christ redeemed us from the curse of the law by becoming a curse for us—for it is written, "Cursed is everyone who is hanged on a tree"— so that in Christ Jesus the blessing of Abraham might come to the Gentiles, so that we might receive the promised Spirit through faith. *– Galatians 3:13-14*

He entered once for all into the holy places, not by means of the blood of goats and calves but by means of His own blood, thus securing an eternal redemption. For if the blood of goats and bulls, and the sprinkling of defiled persons with the ashes of a heifer, sanctify for the purification of the flesh, how much more will the blood of Christ, who through the eternal Spirit offered Himself without blemish to God, purify our conscience from dead works to serve the living God. Therefore He is the mediator of a new covenant, so that those who are called may receive the promised eternal inheritance, since a death has occurred that redeems them from the transgressions committed under the first covenant. *– Hebrews 9:12-15*

For the grace of God has appeared, bringing salvation for all people, training us to renounce ungodliness and worldly passions, and to live self-controlled, upright, and godly lives in the present age, waiting for our blessed hope, the appearing of the glory of our great God and Savior Jesus Christ, who gave Himself for us to redeem us from all lawlessness and to purify for Himself a people for His own possession who are zealous for good works. Declare these things; exhort and rebuke with all authority. Let no one disregard you. *– Titus 2:11-15*

Truth and Lies

Take a moment to pray and invite God to meet with you in this process. Reflect on the previous verses, and ask the Holy Spirit to reveal the truth of what God is saying in these Scriptures.

List the truth that was revealed to you:_____

_____

_____

_____

_____

Review the previous verses and ask the Lord to reveal any of your thoughts or feelings that may be opposed to the truth in those Scriptures.

Now ask the Lord what lies you believe that are connected to those thoughts and feelings.

List the lies that were revealed:_____

_____

_____

_____

Forgiveness and Repentance

As you review this list, ask the Lord if there is anyone you need to forgive that may have taught you, or hurt you with, these lies.

"In Jesus' name, I choose to forgive _____ for 'teaching me' or 'hurting me with' the lie that _____."

"In Jesus' name, I break agreement and renounce the lie that _____."

"Jesus, I come into agreement with Your forgiveness, and I completely forgive myself for any way I believed those lies. I release all those lies to You."

Statement of Faith

I have redemption in Jesus through His blood. My sins have been forgiven according to the riches of His grace. God lavished all this upon me, in all wisdom and insight, making known to me the mystery of His will, according to His purpose, which He set forth in Christ. Christ redeemed me from the curse of the law by becoming a curse for me. In Christ Jesus, the blessing of Abraham came to me, so that I could receive the promised Spirit through faith. Jesus is the mediator of a new covenant for me. He called me and gave me the promised eternal inheritance. Jesus gave Himself for me to redeem me from all lawlessness and to purify me for Himself.

Now that you have forgiven, renounced the lies, and read the Statement of Faith, ask God: "What truths about my identity, according to those Scriptures, do You want me to know?"

_____

_____

_____

_____

_____

Let yourself dream, and ask God: "How could believing these truths affect my life?"

_____

_____

_____

_____

_____

Ask God: "What are some practical steps I can take to experience these truths in my life?"

_____

_____

_____

_____

_____

Now ask the Holy Spirit to empower you and make these truths more real in your life.

Identity

Take a moment to pray and reflect on these God-given aspects of your identity:

Saved

Redeemed

Forgiven

Redeemed from the curse

Eternally secure

Called

Purified for Him

His possession

Redeemed from all lawlessness

Zealous for good works

Write down a statement of faith of your own:

_____

_____

_____

_____

_____

Additional thoughts for the day:

_____

_____

_____

_____

_____

_____

_____

_____

_____

Day 2

Are You Justified?

You have freely been rendered and declared righteous and just, by His grace, as the Lord says you ought to be.

For there is no distinction: for all have sinned and fall short of the glory of God, and are justified by His grace as a gift, through the redemption that is in Christ Jesus, whom God put forward as a propitiation by His blood, to be received by faith. This was to show God's righteousness, because in His divine forbearance He had passed over former sins. It was to show His righteousness at the present time, so that He might be just and the justifier of the one who has faith in Jesus. *– Romans 3:22b-26*

Therefore, since we have been justified by faith, we have peace with God through our Lord Jesus Christ. Through Him we have also obtained access by faith into this grace in which we stand, and we rejoice in hope of the glory of God. Not only that, but we rejoice in our sufferings, knowing that suffering produces endurance, and endurance produces character, and character produces hope, and hope does not put us to shame, because God's love has been poured into our hearts through the Holy Spirit who has been given to us. For while we were still weak, at the right time Christ died for the ungodly. For one will scarcely die for a righteous person—though perhaps for a good person one would dare even to die—but God shows His love for us in that while we were still sinners, Christ died for us. Since, therefore, we have now been justified by His blood, much more shall we be saved by Him from the wrath of God. For if while we were enemies we were reconciled to God by the death of His Son, much more, now that we are reconciled, shall we be saved by His life. *– Romans 5:1-10*

But when the goodness and loving kindness of God our Savior appeared, He saved us, not because of works done by us in righteousness, but according to His own mercy, by the washing of regeneration and renewal of the Holy Spirit, whom He poured out on us richly through Jesus Christ our Savior, so that being justified by His grace we might become heirs according to the hope of eternal life. *– Titus 3:4-7*

Truth and Lies

Take a moment to pray and invite God to meet with you in this process. Reflect on the previous verses, and ask the Holy Spirit to reveal the truth of what God is saying in these Scriptures.

List the truth that was revealed to you:_____

_____

_____

_____

_____

Review the previous verses and ask the Lord to reveal any of your thoughts or feelings that may be opposed to the truth in those Scriptures.

Now ask the Lord what lies you believe that are connected to those thoughts and feelings.

List the lies that were revealed:_____

_____

_____

_____

Forgiveness and Repentance

As you review this list, ask the Lord if there is anyone you need to forgive that may have taught you, or hurt you with, these lies.

"In Jesus' name, I choose to forgive _____ for 'teaching me' or 'hurting me with' the lie that _____."

"In Jesus' name, I break agreement and renounce the lie that _____."

"Jesus, I come into agreement with Your forgiveness, and I completely forgive myself for any way I believed those lies. I release all those lies to You."

Statement of Faith

God demonstrates His righteousness by being my justifier. I have been justified freely by God's grace, through the redemption that is in Christ Jesus. Therefore, since I am justified by faith, I have peace with God through our Lord Jesus Christ. I am an heir according to the hope of eternal life by the blood of Jesus.

Now that you have forgiven, renounced the lies, and read the Statement of Faith, ask God: "What truths about my identity, according to those Scriptures, do You want me to know?"

_____

_____

_____

_____

_____

Let yourself dream, and ask God: "How could believing these truths affect my life?"

_____

_____

_____

_____

_____

Ask God: "What are some practical steps I can take to experience these truths in my life?"

_____

_____

_____

_____

Now ask the Holy Spirit to empower you and make these truths more real in your life.

Identity

Take a moment to pray and reflect on these God-given aspects of your identity:

Justified by His grace

Redeemed in Christ Jesus

Standing in grace

Justified by faith

At peace with God

Rejoicing in hope

Not put to shame

An heir according to the hope of eternal life

Loved

Saved by Him

Saved by His life

Saved according to His own mercy

Washed

Regenerated

Renewed

Justified by His blood

Write down a statement of faith of your own:

_____

_____

_____

_____

_____

_____

Additional thoughts for the day:

_____

_____

_____

Day 3

Are You Sanctified?

You have been declared holy and pure. You have been dedicated to God through the sacrifice of Christ Jesus.

They are not of the world, just as I am not of the world. Sanctify them in the truth; Your word is truth. As You sent Me into the world, so I have sent them into the world. And for their sake I consecrate Myself, that they also may be sanctified in truth. *- John 17:16-19*

Now may the God of peace Himself sanctify you completely, and may your whole spirit and soul and body be kept blameless at the coming of our Lord Jesus Christ. He who calls you is faithful; He will surely do it. *- 1 Thessalonians 5:23-24*

Consequently, when Christ came into the world, He said, "Sacrifices and offerings You have not desired, but a body have You prepared for me; in burnt offerings and sin offerings You have taken no pleasure. Then I said, 'Behold, I have come to do Your will, O God, as it is written of Me in the scroll of the book.' " When He said above, "You have neither desired nor taken pleasure in sacrifices and offerings and burnt offerings and sin offerings" (these are offered according to the law), then He added, "Behold, I have come to do Your will." He does away with the first in order to establish the second. And by that will we have been sanctified through the offering of the body of Jesus Christ once for all. And every priest stands daily at his service, offering repeatedly the same sacrifices, which can never take away sins. But when Christ had offered for all time a single sacrifice for sins, He sat down at the right hand of God, waiting from that time until His enemies should be made a footstool for His feet. For by a single offering He has perfected for all time those who are being sanctified. And the Holy Spirit also bears witness to us; for after saying, "This is the covenant that I will make with them after those days, declares the Lord: I will put My laws on their hearts, and write them on their minds," then He adds, "I will remember their sins and their lawless deeds no more." Where there is forgiveness of these, there is no longer any offering for sin. *- Hebrews 10:5-18*

Truth and Lies

Take a moment to pray and invite God to meet with you in this process. Reflect on the previous verses, and ask the Holy Spirit to reveal the truth of what God is saying in these Scriptures.

List the truth that was revealed to you:_____

_____

_____

_____

_____

Review the previous verses and ask the Lord to reveal any of your thoughts or feelings that may be opposed to the truth in those Scriptures.

Now ask the Lord what lies you believe that are connected to those thoughts and feelings.

List the lies that were revealed:_____

_____

_____

_____

Forgiveness and Repentance

As you review this list, ask the Lord if there is anyone you need to forgive that may have taught you, or hurt you with, these lies.

"In Jesus' name, I choose to forgive _____ for 'teaching me' or 'hurting me with' the lie that _____."

"In Jesus' name, I break agreement and renounce the lie that _____."

"Jesus, I come into agreement with Your forgiveness, and I completely forgive myself for any way I believed those lies. I release all those lies to You."

15

Statement of Faith

I have been sanctified in the truth; Your Word is truth. God Himself, the God of peace, sanctifies me completely. He has perfected me for all time, through the single offering of Jesus Christ.

Now that you have forgiven, renounced the lies, and read the Statement of Faith, ask God: "What truths about my identity, according to those Scriptures, do You want me to know?"

_____

_____

_____

_____

_____

Let yourself dream, and ask God: "How could believing these truths affect my life?"

_____

_____

_____

_____

_____

Ask God: "What are some practical steps I can take to experience these truths in my life?"

_____

_____

_____

_____

_____

Now ask the Holy Spirit to empower you and make these truths more real in your life.

Identity

Take a moment to pray and reflect on these God-given aspects of your identity:

Not of the world

Sent by Jesus

Called

Sanctified in truth

Kept blameless

Sanctified through the offering of Jesus Christ

Sanctified completely

Perfected for all time

Write down a statement of faith of your own:

_____

_____

_____

_____

_____

_____

Additional thoughts for the day:

_____

_____

_____

_____

_____

_____

_____

_____

Day 4

Are You Reconciled?

For freedom, Christ has set you free. You are a new creation. The old has passed and the new has come. All this is from God, who has received you into favor, restored you, and brought you into proper and right relationship with Him.

Already you are clean because of the word that I have spoken to you. – *John 15:3*

But thanks be to God, that you who were once slaves of sin have become obedient from the heart to the standard of teaching to which you were committed, and, having been set free from sin, have become slaves of righteousness. – *Romans 6:17-18*

Therefore, if anyone is in Christ, he is a new creation. The old has passed away; behold, the new has come. All this is from God, who through Christ reconciled us to Himself and gave us the ministry of reconciliation. – *2 Corinthians 5:17-18*

For freedom Christ has set us free; stand firm therefore, and do not submit again to a yoke of slavery. – *Galatians 5:1*

But God, being rich in mercy, because of the great love with which He loved us, even when we were dead in our trespasses, made us alive together with Christ—by grace you have been saved—and raised us up with Him and seated us with Him in the heavenly places in Christ Jesus. – *Ephesians 2:4-6*

But now in Christ Jesus you who once were far off have been brought near by the blood of Christ. – *Ephesians 2:13*

So then you are no longer strangers and aliens, but you are fellow citizens with the saints and members of the household of God, built on the foundation of the apostles and prophets, Christ Jesus Himself being the cornerstone. – *Ephesians 2:19-20*

And you, who once were alienated and hostile in mind, doing evil deeds, He has now reconciled in His body of flesh by His death, in order to present you holy and blameless and above reproach before Him. – *Colossians 1:21-22*

Truth and Lies

Take a moment to pray and invite God to meet with you in this process. Reflect on the previous verses, and ask the Holy Spirit to reveal the truth of what God is saying in these Scriptures.

List the truth that was revealed to you:_____

_____

_____

_____

_____

Review the previous verses and ask the Lord to reveal any of your thoughts or feelings that may be opposed to the truth in those Scriptures.

Now ask the Lord what lies you believe that are connected to those thoughts and feelings.

List the lies that were revealed:_____

_____

_____

_____

Forgiveness and Repentance

As you review this list, ask the Lord if there is anyone you need to forgive that may have taught you, or hurt you with, these lies.

"In Jesus' name, I choose to forgive _____ for 'teaching me' or 'hurting me with' the lie that _____."

"In Jesus' name, I break agreement and renounce the lie that _____."

"Jesus, I come into agreement with Your forgiveness, and I completely forgive myself for any way I believed those lies. I release all those lies to You."

Statement of Faith

I am saved by grace and made alive together with Christ. God has raised me up with Christ and seated me with Him in heavenly places. Through the blood of Jesus Christ, He brought me near to Himself. I have been set free from sin and have become a slave to righteousness. For freedom, Christ has set me free. I am clean because of the word Jesus spoke over me. He reconciled me through His body, and now presents me holy, blameless, and free from accusation. I am a new creation in Christ. The old is gone and the new has come. All this is from God, who reconciled me to Himself, and made me a member of His household. God created me in Christ Jesus for good works.

Now that you have forgiven, renounced the lies, and read the Statement of Faith, ask God: "What truths about my identity, according to those Scriptures, do You want me to know?"

_____

_____

_____

_____

_____

Let yourself dream, and ask God: "How could believing these truths affect my life?"

_____

_____

_____

_____

_____

Ask God: "What are some practical steps I can take to experience these truths in my life?"

_____

_____

_____

_____

_____

Now ask the Holy Spirit to empower you and make these truths more real in your life.

Identity

Take a moment to pray and reflect on these God-given aspects of your identity:

Clean	Loved	Saved
Obedient from the heart	Alive together with Christ	Reconciled in His body
Set free from sin	Raised up with Him	A minister of reconciliation
A slave of righteousness	Seated with Him	Blameless
A new creation	Brought near	Above reproach before Him
Reconciled to Him	Holy	
Free	A member of God's household	A fellow citizen

Write down a statement of faith of your own:

_____

_____

_____

_____

_____

_____

Additional thoughts for the day:

_____

_____

_____

_____

_____

_____

_____

_____

Day 5

Are You Dead To Sin?

You know that your old self was crucified with Christ in order that your body of sin might be rendered inactive, destroyed, made completely inoperative, and done away with, so that you could be completely severed from it, no longer enslaved to sin.

I have been crucified with Christ. It is no longer I who live, but Christ who lives in me. And the life I now live in the flesh I live by faith in the Son of God, who loved me and gave Himself for me. – *Galatians 2:20*

If then you have been raised with Christ, seek the things that are above, where Christ is, seated at the right hand of God. Set your minds on things that are above, not on things that are on earth. For you have died, and your life is hidden with Christ in God. – *Colossians 3:1-3*

For God has done what the law, weakened by the flesh, could not do. By sending His own Son in the likeness of sinful flesh and for sin, He condemned sin in the flesh. – *Romans 8:3*

What shall we say then? Are we to continue in sin that grace may abound? By no means! How can we who died to sin still live in it? Do you not know that all of us who have been baptized into Christ Jesus were baptized into His death? We were buried therefore with Him by baptism into death, in order that, just as Christ was raised from the dead by the glory of the Father, we too might walk in newness of life. For if we have been united with Him in a death like His, we shall certainly be united with Him in a resurrection like His. We know that our old self was crucified with Him in order that the body of sin might be brought to nothing, so that we would no longer be enslaved to sin. For one who has died has been set free from sin. Now if we have died with Christ, we believe that we will also live with Him. We know that Christ, being raised from the dead, will never die again; death no longer has dominion over Him. For the death He died He died to sin, once for all, but the life He lives He lives to God. So you also must consider yourselves dead to sin and alive to God in Christ Jesus. – *Romans 6:1-11*

Truth and Lies

Take a moment to pray and invite God to meet with you in this process. Reflect on the previous verses, and ask the Holy Spirit to reveal the truth of what God is saying in these Scriptures.

List the truth that was revealed to you:_____

_____

_____

_____

_____

Review the previous verses and ask the Lord to reveal any of your thoughts or feelings that may be opposed to the truth in those Scriptures.

Now ask the Lord what lies you believe that are connected to those thoughts and feelings.

List the lies that were revealed:_____

_____

_____

_____

_____

Forgiveness and Repentance

As you review this list, ask the Lord if there is anyone you need to forgive that may have taught you, or hurt you with, these lies.

"In Jesus' name, I choose to forgive _____ for 'teaching me' or 'hurting me with' the lie that _____."

"In Jesus' name, I break agreement and renounce the lie that _____."

"Jesus, I come into agreement with Your forgiveness, and I completely forgive myself for any way I believed those lies. I release all those lies to You."

Statement of Faith

My old self has been crucified with Christ. When I was still just a sinner, Jesus condemned sin in my flesh so that my old body of sin was brought to nothing. I was united with Him in His death and buried with Him in baptism. I am dead to sin, no longer a slave to sin, and I have been set free from sin in Christ Jesus.

Now that you have forgiven, renounced the lies, and read the Statement of Faith, ask God: "What truths about my identity, according to those Scriptures, do You want me to know?"

_____

_____

_____

_____

Let yourself dream, and ask God: "How could believing these truths affect my life?"

_____

_____

_____

_____

Ask God: "What are some practical steps I can take to experience these truths in my life?"

_____

_____

_____

_____

Now ask the Holy Spirit to empower you and make these truths more real in your life.

Identity

Take a moment to pray and reflect on these God-given aspects of your identity:

Crucified with Christ

Baptized into Christ Jesus

Hidden with Christ in God

Dead to sin

United with Him in resurrection

No longer enslaved to sin

Set free from sin

Loved

Raised with Christ

Write down a statement of faith of your own:

_____

_____

_____

_____

_____

_____

Additional thoughts for the day:

_____

_____

_____

_____

_____

Day 6

Are You Alive In The Spirit?

By grace through faith you are forgiven, redeemed, reconciled, washed clean, justified, sanctified, set free, righteous, saved, healed, delivered, made whole, alive, and united with Jesus in life to live for God.

Therefore, as one trespass led to condemnation for all men, so one act of righteousness leads to justification and life for all men. For as by the one man's disobedience the many were made sinners, so by the one man's obedience the many will be made righteous. Now the law came in to increase the trespass, but where sin increased, grace abounded all the more, so that, as sin reigned in death, grace also might reign through righteousness leading to eternal life through Jesus Christ our Lord. *– Romans 5:18-21*

We were buried therefore with Him by baptism into death, in order that, just as Christ was raised from the dead by the glory of the Father, we too might walk in newness of life. For if we have been united with Him in a death like His, we shall certainly be united with Him in a resurrection like His. *– Romans 6:4-5*

But now that you have been set free from sin and have become slaves of God, the fruit you get leads to sanctification and its end, eternal life. For the wages of sin is death, but the free gift of God is eternal life in Christ Jesus our Lord. *– Romans 6:22-23*

If the Spirit of Him who raised Jesus from the dead dwells in you, He who raised Christ Jesus from the dead will also give life to your mortal bodies through His Spirit who dwells in you. *– Romans 8:11*

Therefore, if anyone is in Christ, he is a new creation. The old has passed away; behold, the new has come. *– 2 Corinthians 5:17*

For through the law I died to the law, so that I might live to God. I have been crucified with Christ. It is no longer I who live, but Christ who lives in me. And the life I now live in the flesh I live by faith in the Son of God, who loved me and gave Himself for me. *– Galatians 2:19-20*

Truth and Lies

Take a moment to pray and invite God to meet with you in this process. Reflect on the previous verses, and ask the Holy Spirit to reveal the truth of what God is saying in these Scriptures.

List the truth that was revealed to you:_____

_____

_____

_____

_____

Review the previous verses and ask the Lord to reveal any of your thoughts or feelings that may be opposed to the truth in those Scriptures.

Now ask the Lord what lies you believe that are connected to those thoughts and feelings.

List the lies that were revealed:_____

_____

_____

_____

Forgiveness and Repentance

As you review this list, ask the Lord if there is anyone you need to forgive that may have taught you, or hurt you with, these lies.

"In Jesus' name, I choose to forgive _____ for 'teaching me' or 'hurting me with' the lie that _____."

"In Jesus' name, I break agreement and renounce the lie that _____."

"Jesus, I come into agreement with Your forgiveness, and I completely forgive myself for any way I believed those lies. I release all those lies to You."

Statement of Faith

By grace, I am united with Christ in His resurrection. It is no longer my old self who lives, but Christ who lives in me. By faith, I am made righteous through Jesus, and I reign with Him in newness of life. The old has passed away and the new has come. I am saved by grace, and grace reigns through me for eternal life. I am a new creation in Christ. I am alive in the Spirit and I live to God.

Now that you have forgiven, renounced the lies, and read the Statement of Faith, ask God: "What truths about my identity, according to those Scriptures, do You want me to know?"

_____

_____

_____

_____

_____

Let yourself dream, and ask God: "How could believing these truths affect my life?"

_____

_____

_____

_____

_____

Ask God: "What are some practical steps I can take to experience these truths in my life?"

_____

_____

_____

_____

_____

Now ask the Holy Spirit to empower you and make these truths more real in your life.

Identity

Take a moment to pray and reflect on these God-given aspects of your identity:

Justified

Alive

Righteous

Walking in newness of life

United with Him

Set free from sin

A slave to God

A new creation

Living to God

Christ in me

Loved

Indwelled with the Spirit

Eternally alive in Christ Jesus

Write down a statement of faith of your own:

_____

_____

_____

_____

_____

Additional thoughts for the day:

_____

_____

_____

Day 7

Is Your Mind Set On The Spirit?

You are not in the flesh; you are in the Spirit. Decide and purpose to count and judge yourself dead to sin and alive to God. You are pleasing to God, and the Spirit dwells in you. Let yourself be filled with the Spirit and live according to the Spirit. Set your mind on the things of the Spirit.

So you also must consider yourselves dead to sin and alive to God in Christ Jesus. – *Romans 6:11*

There is therefore now no condemnation for those who are in Christ Jesus. For the law of the Spirit of life has set you free in Christ Jesus from the law of sin and death. For God has done what the law, weakened by the flesh, could not do. By sending His own Son in the likeness of sinful flesh and for sin, He condemned sin in the flesh, in order that the righteous requirement of the law might be fulfilled in us, who walk not according to the flesh but according to the Spirit. For those who live according to the flesh set their minds on the things of the flesh, but those who live according to the Spirit set their minds on the things of the Spirit. For to set the mind on the flesh is death, but to set the mind on the Spirit is life and peace. For the mind that is set on the flesh is hostile to God, for it does not submit to God's law; indeed, it cannot. Those who are in the flesh cannot please God. You, however, are not in the flesh but in the Spirit, if in fact the Spirit of God dwells in you. Anyone who does not have the Spirit of Christ does not belong to Him. But if Christ is in you, although the body is dead because of sin, the Spirit is life because of righteousness. – *Romans 8:1-10*

And do not get drunk with wine, for that is debauchery, but be filled with the Spirit. – *Ephesians 5:18*

If then you have been raised with Christ, seek the things that are above, where Christ is, seated at the right hand of God. Set your minds on things that are above, not on things that are on earth. For you have died, and your life is hidden with Christ in God. When Christ who is your life appears, then you also will appear with Him in glory. – *Colossians 3:1-4*

Truth and Lies

Take a moment to pray and invite God to meet with you in this process. Reflect on the previous verses, and ask the Holy Spirit to reveal the truth of what God is saying in these Scriptures.

List the truth that was revealed to you:_____

_____

_____

_____

_____

Review the previous verses and ask the Lord to reveal any of your thoughts or feelings that may be opposed to the truth in those Scriptures.

Now ask the Lord what lies you believe that are connected to those thoughts and feelings.

List the lies that were revealed:_____

_____

_____

_____

Forgiveness and Repentance

As you review this list, ask the Lord if there is anyone you need to forgive that may have taught you, or hurt you with, these lies.

"In Jesus' name, I choose to forgive _____ for 'teaching me' or 'hurting me with' the lie that _____."

"In Jesus' name, I break agreement and renounce the lie that _____."

"Jesus, I come into agreement with Your forgiveness, and I completely forgive myself for any way I believed those lies. I release all those lies to You."

Statement of Faith

I am set free in Christ, and my life is hidden with Him in God. I am not in the flesh, I am not controlled by the flesh, and I do not live according to the flesh. I am in the Spirit and live according to the Spirit. The Spirit dwells in me and gives me life. I am alive to God and I belong to Christ Jesus. He lives in me, and I have life and peace because my mind is set on the things of the Spirit.

Now that you have forgiven, renounced the lies, and read the Statement of Faith, ask God: "What truths about my identity, according to those Scriptures, do You want me to know?"

_____

_____

_____

_____

_____

Let yourself dream, and ask God: "How could believing these truths affect my life?"

_____

_____

_____

_____

_____

Ask God: "What are some practical steps I can take to experience these truths in my life?"

_____

_____

_____

_____

_____

Now ask the Holy Spirit to empower you and make these truths more real in your life.

Identity

Take a moment to pray and reflect on these God-given aspects of your identity:

Dead to sin

Alive to God

In Christ Jesus

Not condemned

Free from the law of sin and death

Set free in Christ

Filled with the righteous requirements of the law

Living according to the Spirit

Set on the things of the Spirit

In glory

In the Spirit

Belonging to Him

Filled with the Spirit

Raised with Christ

Hidden with Christ in God

Write down a statement of faith of your own:

_____

_____

_____

_____

_____

_____

Additional thoughts for the day:

_____

_____

_____

_____

_____

_____

_____

_____

Day 8

Are You Renewed?

I appeal to you therefore, brothers, by the deep longing, compassion, and mercies of God, to present your bodies as a living sacrifice, holy and acceptable to God, which is your reasonable, logical, and spiritual act of service and worship to Him. Do not be conformed to this world, but be transformed by the renewal of your mind, that you may recognize the genuine will of God, and then approve and prove what is good and acceptable and perfect.

Let not sin therefore reign in your mortal body, to make you obey its passions. Do not present your members to sin as instruments for unrighteousness, but present yourselves to God as those who have been brought from death to life, and your members to God as instruments for righteousness. *– Romans 6:12-13*

Now this I say and testify in the Lord, that you must no longer walk as the Gentiles do, in the futility of their minds. They are darkened in their understanding, alienated from the life of God because of the ignorance that is in them, due to their hardness of heart. They have become callous and have given themselves up to sensuality, greedy to practice every kind of impurity. But that is not the way you learned Christ!—assuming that you have heard about Him and were taught in Him, as the truth is in Jesus, to put off your old self, which belongs to your former manner of life and is corrupt through deceitful desires, and to be renewed in the spirit of your minds, and to put on the new self, created after the likeness of God in true righteousness and holiness. *– Ephesians 4:17-24*

Do not lie to one another, seeing that you have put off the old self with its practices and have put on the new self, which is being renewed in knowledge after the image of its Creator. Here there is not Greek and Jew, circumcised and uncircumcised, barbarian, Scythian, slave, free; but Christ is all, and in all. *– Colossians 3:9-11*

Do your best to present yourself to God as one approved, a worker who has no need to be ashamed, rightly handling the word of truth. *– 2 Timothy 2:15*

I appeal to you therefore, brothers, by the mercies of God, to present your bodies as a living sacrifice, holy and acceptable to God, which is your spiritual worship. Do not be conformed to this world, but be transformed by the renewal of your mind, that by testing you may discern what is the will of God, what is good and acceptable and perfect. *– Romans 12:1-2*

Truth and Lies

Take a moment to pray and invite God to meet with you in this process. Reflect on the previous verses, and ask the Holy Spirit to reveal the truth of what God is saying in these Scriptures.

List the truth that was revealed to you:_____

_____

_____

_____

_____

Review the previous verses and ask the Lord to reveal any of your thoughts or feelings that may be opposed to the truth in those Scriptures.

Now ask the Lord what lies you believe that are connected to those thoughts and feelings.

List the lies that were revealed:_____

_____

_____

_____

Forgiveness and Repentance

As you review this list, ask the Lord if there is anyone you need to forgive that may have taught you, or hurt you with, these lies.

"In Jesus' name, I choose to forgive _____ for 'teaching me' or 'hurting me with' the lie that _____."

"In Jesus' name, I break agreement and renounce the lie that _____."

"Jesus, I come into agreement with Your forgiveness, and I completely forgive myself for any way I believed those lies. I release all those lies to You."

Statement of Faith

I have been brought from death to life. All of me is new. I have been created after the likeness of God as an instrument of true righteousness and holiness. I am an approved, holy, and acceptable living sacrifice, being renewed in the knowledge of my Creator. I can discern the will of God – what is His good, acceptable, and perfect will.

Now that you have forgiven, renounced the lies, and read the Statement of Faith, ask God: "What truths about my identity, according to those Scriptures, do You want me to know?"

_____

_____

_____

_____

_____

Let yourself dream, and ask God: "How could believing these truths affect my life?"

_____

_____

_____

_____

_____

Ask God: "What are some practical steps I can take to experience these truths in my life?"

_____

_____

_____

_____

_____

Now ask the Holy Spirit to empower you and make these truths more real in your life.

Identity

Take a moment to pray and reflect on these God-given aspects of your identity:

Brought from death to life

An instrument for righteousness

Renewed

Created in true righteousness and true holiness

New

Renewed in knowledge after the image of my Creator

Unashamed

A living sacrifice

Holy

Created after the likeness of God

An approved worker

Acceptable to God

Able to discern the will of God

Write down a statement of faith of your own:

_____

_____

_____

_____

_____

Additional thoughts for the day:

_____

_____

Day 9

Are You Righteous?

Now that you have put your faith in Jesus, you are as you ought to be. You are right with God, acceptable, approved, virtuous, and pure in life, apart from the law. You are blessed, and your sins will never be counted against you.

But now the righteousness of God has been manifested apart from the law, although the Law and the Prophets bear witness to it—the righteousness of God through faith in Jesus Christ for all who believe. For there is no distinction: for all have sinned and fall short of the glory of God, and are justified by His grace as a gift, through the redemption that is in Christ Jesus. - *Romans 3:21-24*

And to the one who does not work but believes in Him who justifies the ungodly, his faith is counted as righteousness, just as David also speaks of the blessing of the one to whom God counts righteousness apart from works: "Blessed are those whose lawless deeds are forgiven, and whose sins are covered; blessed is the man against whom the Lord will not count his sin." - *Romans 4:5-8*

For the promise to Abraham and his offspring that he would be heir of the world did not come through the law but through the righteousness of faith. - *Romans 4:13*

That is why it depends on faith, in order that the promise may rest on grace and be guaranteed to all his offspring—not only to the adherent of the law but also to the one who shares the faith of Abraham, who is the father of us all. - *Romans 4:16*

But thanks be to God, that you who were once slaves of sin have become obedient from the heart to the standard of teaching to which you were committed, and, having been set free from sin, have become slaves of righteousness. - *Romans 6:17-18*

And because of Him you are in Christ Jesus, who became to us wisdom from God, righteousness and sanctification and redemption. - *1 Corinthians 1:30*

For our sake He made Him to be sin who knew no sin, so that in Him we might become the righteousness of God. - *2 Corinthians 5:21*

Truth and Lies

Take a moment to pray and invite God to meet with you in this process. Reflect on the previous verses, and ask the Holy Spirit to reveal the truth of what God is saying in these Scriptures.

List the truth that was revealed to you:_____

_____

_____

_____

_____

Review the previous verses and ask the Lord to reveal any of your thoughts or feelings that may be opposed to the truth in those Scriptures.

Now ask the Lord what lies you believe that are connected to those thoughts and feelings.

List the lies that were revealed:_____

_____

_____

_____

Forgiveness and Repentance

As you review this list, ask the Lord if there is anyone you need to forgive that may have taught you, or hurt you with, these lies.

"In Jesus' name, I choose to forgive _____ for 'teaching me' or 'hurting me with' the lie that _____."

"In Jesus' name, I break agreement and renounce the lie that _____."

"Jesus, I come into agreement with Your forgiveness, and I completely forgive myself for any way I believed those lies. I release all those lies to You."

Statement of Faith

By faith, as an offspring of Abraham, I am guaranteed to be an heir of the promise. I am in Christ. God is my wisdom, righteousness, sanctification, and redemption. I have become the righteousness of God in Jesus Christ. I am blessed. My sins are forgiven, covered, and will never be counted against me.

Now that you have forgiven, renounced the lies, and read the Statement of Faith, ask God: "What truths about my identity, according to those Scriptures, do You want me to know?"

_____

_____

_____

_____

Let yourself dream, and ask God: "How could believing these truths affect my life?"

_____

_____

_____

_____

Ask God: "What are some practical steps I can take to experience these truths in my life?"

_____

_____

_____

_____

Now ask the Holy Spirit to empower you and make these truths more real in your life.

Identity

Take a moment to pray and reflect on these God-given aspects of your identity:

Justified by His grace

Redeemed

Righteous apart from works

A guaranteed heir of the promise

Forgiven

Covered

Abraham's offspring

Obedient from the heart

Set free from sin

A slave of righteousness

In Christ

Sanctified

The righteousness of God

Write down a statement of faith of your own:

_____

_____

_____

_____

_____

Additional thoughts for the day:

_____

_____

_____

_____

Day 10

Is The Law Fulfilled In You?

God sent His Son, in the likeness of sinful flesh, to condemn sin in the flesh. He did this in order that the righteous requirements of the law could be made perfect and complete in you. You are filled, to the full, with these righteous requirements, and He will accomplish them. He will bring them into realization in your life, while you walk according to the Spirit.

There is therefore now no condemnation for those who are in Christ Jesus. For the law of the Spirit of life has set you free in Christ Jesus from the law of sin and death. For God has done what the law, weakened by the flesh, could not do. By sending His own Son in the likeness of sinful flesh and for sin, He condemned sin in the flesh, in order that the righteous requirement of the law might be fulfilled in us, who walk not according to the flesh but according to the Spirit. For those who live according to the flesh set their minds on the things of the flesh, but those who live according to the Spirit set their minds on the things of the Spirit. For to set the mind on the flesh is death, but to set the mind on the Spirit is life and peace. For the mind that is set on the flesh is hostile to God, for it does not submit to God's law; indeed, it cannot. Those who are in the flesh cannot please God. You, however, are not in the flesh but in the Spirit, if in fact the Spirit of God dwells in you. Anyone who does not have the Spirit of Christ does not belong to Him. But if Christ is in you, although the body is dead because of sin, the Spirit is life because of righteousness. If the Spirit of Him who raised Jesus from the dead dwells in you, He who raised Christ Jesus from the dead will also give life to your mortal bodies through His Spirit who dwells in you. So then, brothers, we are debtors, not to the flesh, to live according to the flesh. For if you live according to the flesh you will die, but if by the Spirit you put to death the deeds of the body, you will live. For all who are led by the Spirit of God are sons of God. For you did not receive the spirit of slavery to fall back into fear, but you have received the Spirit of adoption as sons, by whom we cry, "Abba! Father!" The Spirit Himself bears witness with our spirit that we are children of God, and if children, then heirs—heirs of God and fellow heirs with Christ, provided we suffer with Him in order that we may also be glorified with Him. *- Romans 8:1-17*

Truth and Lies

Take a moment to pray and invite God to meet with you in this process. Reflect on the previous verses, and ask the Holy Spirit to reveal the truth of what God is saying in these Scriptures.

List the truth that was revealed to you:_____

_____

_____

_____

_____

Review the previous verses and ask the Lord to reveal any of your thoughts or feelings that may be opposed to the truth in those Scriptures.

Now ask the Lord what lies you believe that are connected to those thoughts and feelings.

List the lies that were revealed:_____

_____

_____

_____

Forgiveness and Repentance

As you review this list, ask the Lord if there is anyone you need to forgive that may have taught you, or hurt you with, these lies.

"In Jesus' name, I choose to forgive _____ for 'teaching me' or 'hurting me with' the lie that _____."

"In Jesus' name, I break agreement and renounce the lie that _____."

"Jesus, I come into agreement with Your forgiveness, and I completely forgive myself for any way I believed those lies. I release all those lies to You."

Statement of Faith

I am in Christ and set free from condemnation. God sent His own Son, in the likeness of sinful flesh, to condemn sin in my flesh. The righteous requirements of the law are fulfilled in me. I walk according to the Spirit, with my mind set on the things of the Spirit. I am in the Spirit, and my mind is filled with life and peace. The Spirit dwells in me, and my spirit is alive because of righteousness.

Now that you have forgiven, renounced the lies, and read the Statement of Faith, ask God: "What truths about my identity, according to those Scriptures, do You want me to know?"

_____

_____

_____

_____

_____

Let yourself dream, and ask God: "How could believing these truths affect my life?"

_____

_____

_____

_____

_____

Ask God: "What are some practical steps I can take to experience these truths in my life?"

_____

_____

_____

_____

_____

Now ask the Holy Spirit to empower you and make these truths more real in your life.

Identity

Take a moment to pray and reflect on these God-given aspects of your identity:

Not condemned

In Christ Jesus

Set free

Filled with the righteous requirements of the law

Walking according to the Spirit

Not in the flesh

Free from the law of sin and death

In the Spirit

Led by the Spirit

A child of God

An heir of God

A fellow heir with Christ

Glorified with Him

Write down a statement of faith of your own:

_____

_____

_____

_____

_____

_____

Additional thoughts for the day:

_____

_____

_____

Day 11

Are You Fruitful?

Y ou are God's workmanship. You were created, in Christ, for good works which He prepared beforehand. He is sure that the works He began in you will be accomplished and completed by Him.

For You formed my inward parts; You knitted me together in my mother's womb. I praise You, for I am fearfully and wonderfully made. Wonderful are Your works; my soul knows it very well.
– *Psalm 139:13-14*

But God, being rich in mercy, because of the great love with which He loved us, even when we were dead in our trespasses, made us alive together with Christ—by grace you have been saved—and raised us up with Him and seated us with Him in the heavenly places in Christ Jesus, so that in the coming ages He might show the immeasurable riches of His grace in kindness toward us in Christ Jesus. For by grace you have been saved through faith. And this is not your own doing; it is the gift of God, not a result of works, so that no one may boast. For we are His workmanship, created in Christ Jesus for good works, which God prepared beforehand, that we should walk in them.
– *Ephesians 2:4-10*

I thank my God in all my remembrance of you, always in every prayer of mine for you all making my prayer with joy, because of your partnership in the gospel from the first day until now. And I am sure of this, that He who began a good work in you will bring it to completion at the day of Jesus Christ. It is right for me to feel this way about you all, because I hold you in my heart, for you are all partakers with me of grace, both in my imprisonment and in the defense and confirmation of the gospel. For God is my witness, how I yearn for you all with the affection of Christ Jesus. And it is my prayer that your love may abound more and more, with knowledge and all discernment, so that you may approve what is excellent, and so be pure and blameless for the day of Christ, filled with the fruit of righteousness that comes through Jesus Christ, to the glory and praise of God. – *Philippians 1:3-11*

Truth and Lies

Take a moment to pray and invite God to meet with you in this process. Reflect on the previous verses, and ask the Holy Spirit to reveal the truth of what God is saying in these Scriptures.

List the truth that was revealed to you:_____

_____

_____

_____

_____

Review the previous verses and ask the Lord to reveal any of your thoughts or feelings that may be opposed to the truth in those Scriptures.

Now ask the Lord what lies you believe that are connected to those thoughts and feelings.

List the lies that were revealed:_____

_____

_____

_____

Forgiveness and Repentance

As you review this list, ask the Lord if there is anyone you need to forgive that may have taught you, or hurt you with, these lies.

"In Jesus' name, I choose to forgive _____ for 'teaching me' or 'hurting me with' the lie that _____."

"In Jesus' name, I break agreement and renounce the lie that _____."

"Jesus, I come into agreement with Your forgiveness, and I completely forgive myself for any way I believed those lies. I release all those lies to You."

Statement of Faith

I am fearfully and wonderfully made in God's image. Before I was even born, God prepared good works for me to walk in. He will bring these to completion. I am a partner with Him in the gospel of grace. I am filled with the fruit of righteousness through Jesus.

Now that you have forgiven, renounced the lies, and read the Statement of Faith, ask God: "What truths about my identity, according to those Scriptures, do You want me to know?"

_____

_____

_____

_____

_____

Let yourself dream, and ask God: "How could believing these truths affect my life?"

_____

_____

_____

_____

_____

Ask God: "What are some practical steps I can take to experience these truths in my life?"

_____

_____

_____

_____

_____

Now ask the Holy Spirit to empower you and make these truths more real in your life.

Identity

Take a moment to pray and reflect on these God-given aspects of your identity:

Fearfully and wonderfully made

Created in Christ Jesus for good works

Abounding in love

A partaker of grace

Pure and blameless for the day of Christ

A partner in the gospel

Filled with the fruit of righteousness

Alive together with Christ

Seated with Him in the heavenly places

Formed by God

Raised up with Him

His workmanship

Write down a statement of faith of your own:

_____

_____

_____

_____

_____

_____

Additional thoughts for the day:

_____

_____

_____

_____

_____

Day 12

Are You Equipped?

God makes all grace abound to you. You are fully pleasing to Him, and have all sufficiency, in all things at all times. You bear fruit and abound in every good work, business, undertaking, accomplishment, and deed that you do. It is God who works in you to will, work, accomplish, and produce for His good pleasure.

And God is able to make all grace abound to you, so that having all sufficiency in all things at all times, you may abound in every good work. *- 2 Corinthians 9:8*

And so, from the day we heard, we have not ceased to pray for you, asking that you may be filled with the knowledge of His will in all spiritual wisdom and understanding, so as to walk in a manner worthy of the Lord, fully pleasing to Him, bearing fruit in every good work and increasing in the knowledge of God. May you be strengthened with all power, according to His glorious might, for all endurance and patience with joy, giving thanks to the Father, who has qualified you to share in the inheritance of the saints in light. *- Colossians 1:9-12*

Now may the God of peace who brought again from the dead our Lord Jesus, the great shepherd of the sheep, by the blood of the eternal covenant, equip you with everything good that you may do His will, working in us that which is pleasing in His sight, through Jesus Christ, to whom be glory forever and ever. Amen. *- Hebrews 13:20-21*

Therefore, my beloved, as you have always obeyed, so now, not only as in my presence but much more in my absence, work out your own salvation with fear and trembling, for it is God who works in you, both to will and to work for His good pleasure. *- Philippians 2:12-13*

To this end we always pray for you, that our God may make you worthy of His calling and may fulfill every resolve for good and every work of faith by His power, so that the name of our Lord Jesus may be glorified in you, and you in Him, according to the grace of our God and the Lord Jesus Christ. *- 2 Thessalonians 1:11-12*

Now may our Lord Jesus Christ Himself, and God our Father, who loved us and gave us eternal comfort and good hope through grace, comfort your hearts and establish them in every good work and word. *- 2 Thessalonians 2:16-17*

Truth and Lies

Take a moment to pray and invite God to meet with you in this process. Reflect on the previous verses, and ask the Holy Spirit to reveal the truth of what God is saying in these Scriptures.

List the truth that was revealed to you:_____

_____

_____

_____

_____

Review the previous verses and ask the Lord to reveal any of your thoughts or feelings that may be opposed to the truth in those Scriptures.

Now ask the Lord what lies you believe that are connected to those thoughts and feelings.

List the lies that were revealed:_____

_____

_____

_____

Forgiveness and Repentance

As you review this list, ask the Lord if there is anyone you need to forgive that may have taught you, or hurt you with, these lies.

"In Jesus' name, I choose to forgive _____ for 'teaching me' or 'hurting me with' the lie that _____."

"In Jesus' name, I break agreement and renounce the lie that _____."

"Jesus, I come into agreement with Your forgiveness, and I completely forgive myself for any way I believed those lies. I release all those lies to You."

Statement of Faith

All grace abounds to me. I have all sufficiency, in all things, at all times, to abound in every good work. I am filled with the knowledge of His will, with all spiritual wisdom and understanding, so that I can walk in a manner worthy of the Lord. I am fully pleasing to Him, bearing fruit in every good work. I am strengthened with all power according to His glorious might. He made me worthy of His calling, and I am qualified and equipped with everything good. God is fulfilling His will in me. He is doing the work He prepared for me, for His good pleasure. Jesus is glorified in me, and I am glorified in Jesus. God loves me and eternally comforts me with hope through grace.

Now that you have forgiven, renounced the lies, and read the Statement of Faith, ask God: "What truths about my identity, according to those Scriptures, do You want me to know?"

_____

_____

_____

_____

_____

Let yourself dream, and ask God: "How could believing these truths affect my life?"

_____

_____

_____

_____

_____

Ask God: "What are some practical steps I can take to experience these truths in my life?"

_____

_____

_____

_____

_____

Now ask the Holy Spirit to empower you and make these truths more real in your life.

Identity

Take a moment to pray and reflect on these God-given aspects of your identity:

Having all sufficiency in all things at all times

Abounding in every good work

Filled with the knowledge of His will

Spiritually wise and understanding

Worthy of the Lord

Fully pleasing to Him

Bearing fruit in every good work

Increasing in the knowledge of God

Strengthened with all power

Qualified to share in the inheritance of the saints in light

Equipped with everything good

Pleasing in His sight

Obedient

Working for His good pleasure

Worthy of His calling

Established in every good work and word

Write down a statement of faith of your own:

_____

_____

_____

_____

_____

_____

Additional thoughts for the day:

_____

_____

_____

_____

_____

_____

_____

_____

_____

Day 13

Are You Living In Faith?

Your work is to trust, be confident in, and have faith in Jesus. Believe that He has crucified your old sinful flesh. Be convinced that your life is a life in Christ, led by the Spirit. Believe that as you walk by the Spirit, as a child of light, the fruit of that light is good, right, and true. Be confident in the grace that is training you to renounce all ungodliness. Trust God that this is true. Walk in the Spirit, and you will not gratify the desires of your old dead flesh.

For to me to live is Christ, and to die is gain. If I am to live in the flesh, that means fruitful labor for me. – *Philippians 1:21-22a*

For in Christ Jesus neither circumcision nor uncircumcision counts for anything, but only faith working through love. – *Galatians 5:6*

But I say, walk by the Spirit, and you will not gratify the desires of the flesh. For the desires of the flesh are against the Spirit, and the desires of the Spirit are against the flesh, for these are opposed to each other, to keep you from doing the things you want to do. But if you are led by the Spirit, you are not under the law. – *Galatians 5:16-18*

But the fruit of the Spirit is love, joy, peace, patience, kindness, goodness, faithfulness, gentleness, self-control; against such things there is no law. And those who belong to Christ Jesus have crucified the flesh with its passions and desires. If we live by the Spirit, let us also keep in step with the Spirit. Let us not become conceited, provoking one another, envying one another. – *Galatians 5:22-26*

For at one time you were darkness, but now you are light in the Lord. Walk as children of light (for the fruit of light is found in all that is good and right and true). – *Ephesians 5:8-9*

For the grace of God has appeared, bringing salvation for all people, training us to renounce ungodliness and worldly passions, and to live self-controlled, upright, and godly lives in the present age, waiting for our blessed hope, the appearing of the glory of our great God and Savior Jesus Christ, who gave Himself for us to redeem us from all lawlessness and to purify for Himself a people for His own possession who are zealous for good works. – *Titus 2:11-14*

Jesus answered them, "This is the work of God, that you believe in Him whom He has sent." – *John 6:29*

Truth and Lies

Take a moment to pray and invite God to meet with you in this process. Reflect on the previous verses, and ask the Holy Spirit to reveal the truth of what God is saying in these Scriptures.

List the truth that was revealed to you:_____

_____

_____

_____

_____

Review the previous verses and ask the Lord to reveal any of your thoughts or feelings that may be opposed to the truth in those Scriptures.

Now ask the Lord what lies you believe that are connected to those thoughts and feelings.

List the lies that were revealed:_____

_____

_____

_____

_____

Forgiveness and Repentance

As you review this list, ask the Lord if there is anyone you need to forgive that may have taught you, or hurt you with, these lies.

"In Jesus' name, I choose to forgive _____ for 'teaching me' or 'hurting me with' the lie that _____."

"In Jesus' name, I break agreement and renounce the lie that _____."

"Jesus, I come into agreement with Your forgiveness, and I completely forgive myself for any way I believed those lies. I release all those lies to You."

Statement of Faith

My flesh, with its passions and desires, has been crucified. I live in Christ. My life in Christ is a life of fruitful labor. My fruitful labor is faith working through love. I walk in the Spirit and I am led by the Spirit. I am a child of light: a good, right, and true light in this world. I live by the Spirit and keep in step with the Spirit. The grace of God is training me to renounce all ungodliness, and live an upright, godly life. Jesus purified me as His own and made me zealous for good works.

Now that you have forgiven, renounced the lies, and read the Statement of Faith, ask God: "What truths about my identity, according to those Scriptures, do You want me to know?"

_____

_____

_____

_____

_____

Let yourself dream, and ask God: "How could believing these truths affect my life?"

_____

_____

_____

_____

_____

Ask God: "What are some practical steps I can take to experience these truths in my life?"

_____

_____

_____

_____

_____

Now ask the Holy Spirit to empower you and make these truths more real in your life.

Identity

Take a moment to pray and reflect on these God-given aspects of your identity:

Fruitful	Self-controlled	Saved
Led by the Spirit	Belonging to Christ Jesus	Upright
Not under the law		Trained to renounce ungodliness
Loving	Living by the Spirit	
Joyful	Keeping in step with the Spirit	Godly in this present age
Peaceful	Light in the Lord	Redeemed from all lawlessness
Patient	A child of light	
Kind	Good	Purified for Him
Faithful	Right	His own possession
Gentle	True	Zealous for good works

Write down a statement of faith of your own:

_____

_____

_____

_____

Additional thoughts for the day:

Day 14

Are You Pure?

You are already clean, pure, and free from corrupt desires, sin, guilt, and falsehood. You are fitted and ready to bear fruit because of the word He spoke to you and over you. Our Savior, Jesus Christ, gave Himself to redeem you, free you from all defilement of sin and fault, purify you from wickedness, set you free from the guilt of sin, consecrate you, pronounce you clean, and dedicate you as His own. Let no one disregard or despise you, including yourself.

Already you are clean because of the word that I have spoken to you. Abide in Me, and I in you. As the branch cannot bear fruit by itself, unless it abides in the vine, neither can you, unless you abide in Me. I am the vine; you are the branches. Whoever abides in Me and I in him, he it is that bears much fruit, for apart from Me you can do nothing. *– John 15:3-5*

Blessed be the God and Father of our Lord Jesus Christ, who has blessed us in Christ with every spiritual blessing in the heavenly places, even as He chose us in Him before the foundation of the world, that we should be holy and blameless before Him. In love He predestined us for adoption as sons through Jesus Christ, according to the purpose of His will, to the praise of His glorious grace, with which He has blessed us in the Beloved. *– Ephesians 1:3-6*

Husbands, love your wives, as Christ loved the church and gave Himself up for her, that He might sanctify her, having cleansed her by the washing of water with the Word, so that He might present the church to Himself in splendor, without spot or wrinkle or any such thing, that she might be holy and without blemish. *– Ephesians 5:25-27*

And you, who once were alienated and hostile in mind, doing evil deeds, He has now reconciled in His body of flesh by His death, in order to present you holy and blameless and above reproach before Him. *– Colossians 1:21-22*

For the grace of God has appeared, bringing salvation for all people, training us to renounce ungodliness and worldly passions, and to live self-controlled, upright, and godly lives in the present age, waiting for our blessed hope, the appearing of the glory of our great God and Savior Jesus Christ, who gave Himself for us to redeem us from all lawlessness and to purify for Himself a people for His own possession who are zealous for good works. Declare these things; exhort and rebuke with all authority. Let no one disregard you. *– Titus 2:11-15*

Truth and Lies

Take a moment to pray and invite God to meet with you in this process. Reflect on the previous verses, and ask the Holy Spirit to reveal the truth of what God is saying in these Scriptures.

List the truth that was revealed to you:_____

_____

_____

_____

_____

Review the previous verses and ask the Lord to reveal any of your thoughts or feelings that may be opposed to the truth in those Scriptures.

Now ask the Lord what lies you believe that are connected to those thoughts and feelings.

List the lies that were revealed:_____

_____

_____

_____

Forgiveness and Repentance

As you review this list, ask the Lord if there is anyone you need to forgive that may have taught you, or hurt you with, these lies.

"In Jesus' name, I choose to forgive _____ for 'teaching me' or 'hurting me with' the lie that _____."

"In Jesus' name, I break agreement and renounce the lie that _____."

"Jesus, I come into agreement with Your forgiveness, and I completely forgive myself for any way I believed those lies. I release all those lies to You."

Statement of Faith

I am God's beloved, purified possession. Jesus gave Himself for me so that I could be spotless, without blemish, and free from accusation. He washed me clean, and sanctified me by the word that He spoke to me and over me. He chose me, in Him, to be holy and blameless. I am holy and blameless. I am a dearly loved saint: a guiltless, faultless, clean, and pure saint.

Now that you have forgiven, renounced the lies, and read the Statement of Faith, ask God: "What truths about my identity, according to those Scriptures, do You want me to know?"

_____

_____

_____

_____

_____

Let yourself dream, and ask God: "How could believing these truths affect my life?"

_____

_____

_____

_____

_____

Ask God: "What are some practical steps I can take to experience these truths in my life?"

_____

_____

_____

_____

_____

Now ask the Holy Spirit to empower you and make these truths more real in your life.

Identity

Take a moment to pray and reflect on these God-given aspects of your identity:

Clean

Blessed in Christ

Chosen in Him

Holy

Blameless

Adopted as a son/daughter

Beloved

Loved

Sanctified

Cleansed

Presented in splendor

Without spot or wrinkle

Without blemish

Above reproach

Saved

Self-controlled

Upright

Redeemed from all lawlessness

Purified for Him

Write down a statement of faith of your own:

_____

_____

_____

_____

_____

Additional thoughts for the day:

_____

_____

_____

_____

_____

_____

_____

_____

Day 15

Are You Kept Pure?

Jesus Himself has established you in holiness and purity. He sanctifies you completely. The God of peace Himself will guard, confirm, sustain, and strengthen you. He will keep your whole spirit, soul, and body guiltless and pure. He who calls you is faithful; He will surely do it.

I give thanks to my God always for you because of the grace of God that was given you in Christ Jesus, that in every way you were enriched in Him in all speech and all knowledge—even as the testimony about Christ was confirmed among you—so that you are not lacking in any gift, as you wait for the revealing of our Lord Jesus Christ, who will sustain you to the end, guiltless in the day of our Lord Jesus Christ. God is faithful, by whom you were called into the fellowship of his Son, Jesus Christ our Lord. *– 1 Corinthians 1:4-9*

And I am sure of this, that He who began a good work in you will bring it to completion at the day of Jesus Christ. *– Philippians 1:6*

For God is my witness, how I yearn for you all with the affection of Christ Jesus. And it is my prayer that your love may abound more and more, with knowledge and all discernment, so that you may approve what is excellent, and so be pure and blameless for the day of Christ, filled with the fruit of righteousness that comes through Jesus Christ, to the glory and praise of God. *– Philippians 1:8-11*

And may the Lord make you increase and abound in love for one another and for all, as we do for you, so that He may establish your hearts blameless in holiness before our God and Father, at the coming of our Lord Jesus with all His saints. *– 1 Thessalonians 3:12-13*

Now may the God of peace Himself sanctify you completely, and may your whole spirit and soul and body be kept blameless at the coming of our Lord Jesus Christ. He who calls you is faithful; He will surely do it. *– 1 Thessalonians 5:23-24*

Now to Him who is able to keep you from stumbling and to present you blameless before the presence of His glory with great joy, to the only God, our Savior, through Jesus Christ our Lord, be glory, majesty, dominion, and authority, before all time and now and forever. Amen. *– Jude 24-25*

Truth and Lies

Take a moment to pray and invite God to meet with you in this process. Reflect on the previous verses, and ask the Holy Spirit to reveal the truth of what God is saying in these Scriptures.

List the truth that was revealed to you:_____

_____

_____

_____

_____

Review the previous verses and ask the Lord to reveal any of your thoughts or feelings that may be opposed to the truth in those Scriptures.

Now ask the Lord what lies you believe that are connected to those thoughts and feelings.

List the lies that were revealed:_____

_____

_____

_____

Forgiveness and Repentance

As you review this list, ask the Lord if there is anyone you need to forgive that may have taught you, or hurt you with, these lies.

"In Jesus' name, I choose to forgive _____ for 'teaching me' or 'hurting me with' the lie that _____."

"In Jesus' name, I break agreement and renounce the lie that _____."

"Jesus, I come into agreement with Your forgiveness, and I completely forgive myself for any way I believed those lies. I release all those lies to You."

Statement of Faith

I was called into fellowship with Jesus. I abound in love, with more and more knowledge and discernment. I am pure, blameless, and filled with the fruit of righteousness. He is completing the good work He started in me, and will sustain me guiltless until the end. The Lord increases my love for all the saints. My heart is established as blameless and holy before God, with all the saints. The God of peace is faithful; He is sanctifying me completely. God is able to keep me from stumbling, and present my whole spirit, soul, and body blameless in His presence.

Now that you have forgiven, renounced the lies, and read the Statement of Faith, ask God: "What truths about my identity, according to those Scriptures, do You want me to know?"

_____

_____

_____

_____

_____

Let yourself dream, and ask God: "How could believing these truths affect my life?"

_____

_____

_____

_____

Ask God: "What are some practical steps I can take to experience these truths in my life?"

_____

_____

_____

_____

_____

Now ask the Holy Spirit to empower you and make these truths more real in your life.

Identity

Take a moment to pray and reflect on these God-given aspects of your identity:

Enriched in Him

Not lacking in any gift

Sustained guiltless to the end

Pure

Blameless

Filled with the fruit of righteousness

Increasing and abounding in love

Sanctified completely

Established in holiness before God

His saint

Kept blameless

Kept from stumbling

Presented blameless

Write down a statement of faith of your own:

_____

_____

_____

_____

_____

_____

Additional thoughts for the day:

_____

_____

_____

_____

_____

_____

_____

_____

_____

Day 16

The New Covenant

By means of His own blood, Jesus is the mediator of a new covenant. He wrote this covenant on your heart and mind. He has secured your redemption and your promised, eternal inheritance. By His single offering, He has purified your conscience, cleansed your heart, and washed your body. Jesus has completely perfected you and sanctified you for all time.

He entered once for all into the holy places, not by means of the blood of goats and calves but by means of His own blood, thus securing an eternal redemption...how much more will the blood of Christ, who through the eternal Spirit offered Himself without blemish to God, purify our conscience from dead works to serve the living God. Therefore He is the mediator of a new covenant, so that those who are called may receive the promised eternal inheritance, since a death has occurred that redeems them from the transgressions committed under the first covenant...For Christ has entered, not into holy places made with hands, which are copies of the true things, but into heaven itself, now to appear in the presence of God on our behalf...so Christ, having been offered once to bear the sins of many, will appear a second time, not to deal with sin but to save those who are eagerly waiting for Him.
- Hebrews 9:12,14-15,24,28

Then He added, "Behold, I have come to do Your will." He does away with the first in order to establish the second. And by that will we have been sanctified through the offering of the body of Jesus Christ once for all...But when Christ had offered for all time a single sacrifice for sins, He sat down at the right hand of God...For by a single offering He has perfected for all time those who are being sanctified. And the Holy Spirit also bears witness to us; for after saying, "This is the covenant that I will make with them after those days, declares the Lord: I will put My laws on their hearts, and write them on their minds," then He adds, "I will remember their sins and their lawless deeds no more." Where there is forgiveness of these, there is no longer any offering for sin. Therefore, brothers, since we have confidence to enter the holy places by the blood of Jesus, by the new and living way that He opened for us through the curtain, that is, through His flesh, and since we have a great priest over the house of God, let us draw near with a true heart in full assurance of faith, with our hearts sprinkled clean from an evil conscience and our bodies washed with pure water.
- Hebrews 10:9-10,12,14-22

Truth and Lies

Take a moment to pray and invite God to meet with you in this process. Reflect on the previous verses, and ask the Holy Spirit to reveal the truth of what God is saying in these Scriptures.

List the truth that was revealed to you: _____

_____

_____

_____

_____

Review the previous verses and ask the Lord to reveal any of your thoughts or feelings that may be opposed to the truth in those Scriptures.

Now ask the Lord what lies you believe that are connected to those thoughts and feelings.

List the lies that were revealed: _____

_____

_____

_____

Forgiveness and Repentance

As you review this list, ask the Lord if there is anyone you need to forgive that may have taught you, or hurt you with, these lies.

"In Jesus' name, I choose to forgive _____ for 'teaching me' or 'hurting me with' the lie that _____."

"In Jesus' name, I break agreement and renounce the lie that _____."

"Jesus, I come into agreement with Your forgiveness, and I completely forgive myself for any way I believed those lies. I release all those lies to You."

Statement of Faith

Jesus has purified my conscience from dead works, and has secured an eternal redemption for me. He mediated a new covenant so that I could receive His promised, eternal inheritance. By the will of God, Jesus' single offering has redeemed me, sanctified me, and perfected me for all time. He appeared on my behalf. God will never again remember my sins and lawless deeds. Jesus has washed my heart and my body clean. He wants me to draw near to Him, with my heart full of the assurance of His faithful promises. God's Word is written on my pure heart and my clean mind. I have confidence to enter the holy places by the blood of Jesus.

Now that you have forgiven, renounced the lies, and read the Statement of Faith, ask God: "What truths about my identity, according to those Scriptures, do You want me to know?"

_____

_____

_____

_____

_____

Let yourself dream, and ask God: "How could believing these truths affect my life?"

_____

_____

_____

_____

_____

Ask God: "What are some practical steps I can take to experience these truths in my life?"

_____

_____

_____

_____

_____

Now ask the Holy Spirit to empower you and make these truths more real in your life.

Identity

Take a moment to pray and reflect on these God-given aspects of your identity:

Eternally redeemed

Pure in conscience

Purified from dead works

Promised an eternal inheritance

Called

Redeemed

Saved

Eagerly waiting for Him

Sanctified

Perfected for all time

A brother/sister

Confident to enter the holy places

True hearted

Fully assured in faith

Clean hearted

Washed with pure water

A servant of the living God

Write down a statement of faith of your own:

_____

_____

_____

_____

_____

_____

Additional thoughts for the day:

_____

_____

_____

_____

_____

_____

_____

_____

_____

Day 17

Do You Have a New Heart?

God is your God, and you belong to Him. He has cleansed you, given you a new heart, and written His laws on your heart and mind. He has given you His Spirit. His Spirit causes you to walk, do, produce, and effectually accomplish the fulfillment of His statutes. By Jesus' single offering, He has perfected you for all time, and will remember your sins no more.

For this is the covenant that I will make with the house of Israel after those days, declares the Lord: I will put My law within them, and I will write it on their hearts. And I will be their God, and they shall be My people. - *Jeremiah 31:33*

And I will give them one heart, and a new spirit I will put within them. I will remove the heart of stone from their flesh and give them a heart of flesh, that they may walk in My statutes and keep My rules and obey them. And they shall be My people, and I will be their God. - *Ezekiel 11:19-20*

I will sprinkle clean water on you, and you shall be clean from all your uncleannesses, and from all your idols I will cleanse you. And I will give you a new heart, and a new spirit I will put within you. And I will remove the heart of stone from your flesh and give you a heart of flesh. And I will put My Spirit within you, and cause you to walk in My statutes and be careful to obey My rules. You shall dwell in the land that I gave to your fathers, and you shall be My people, and I will be your God. - *Ezekiel 36:25-28*

For this is the covenant that I will make with the house of Israel after those days, declares the Lord: I will put My laws into their minds, and write them on their hearts, and I will be their God, and they shall be My people. - *Hebrews 8:10*

But when Christ had offered for all time a single sacrifice for sins, He sat down at the right hand of God...For by a single offering He has perfected for all time those who are being sanctified...Then He adds, "I will remember their sins and their lawless deeds no more." - *Hebrews 10:12,14,17*

You yourselves are our letter of recommendation, written on our hearts, to be known and read by all. And you show that you are a letter from Christ delivered by us, written not with ink but with the Spirit of the living God, not on tablets of stone but on tablets of human hearts. - *2 Corinthians 3:2-3*

Truth and Lies

Take a moment to pray and invite God to meet with you in this process. Reflect on the previous verses, and ask the Holy Spirit to reveal the truth of what God is saying in these Scriptures.

List the truth that was revealed to you:_____

_____

_____

_____

_____

Review the previous verses and ask the Lord to reveal any of your thoughts or feelings that may be opposed to the truth in those Scriptures.

Now ask the Lord what lies you believe that are connected to those thoughts and feelings.

List the lies that were revealed:_____

_____

_____

_____

Forgiveness and Repentance

As you review this list, ask the Lord if there is anyone you need to forgive that may have taught you, or hurt you with, these lies.

"In Jesus' name, I choose to forgive _____ for 'teaching me' or 'hurting me with' the lie that _____."

"In Jesus' name, I break agreement and renounce the lie that _____."

"Jesus, I come into agreement with Your forgiveness, and I completely forgive myself for any way I believed those lies. I release all those lies to You."

Statement of Faith

God is my God, and I belong to Him. He has cleansed me and removed all my false idols. By Jesus' single offering, He has forgiven all of my sins and will remember them no more. He has removed my old heart of stone, and given me a new heart of flesh. He has written His laws on my mind and my heart. Jesus has given me a new spirit and has perfected me for all time. His Holy Spirit empowers me to walk in His statutes. I am a letter from Christ, written with the Spirit of the living God, on the tablet of my heart.

Now that you have forgiven, renounced the lies, and read the Statement of Faith, ask God: "What truths about my identity, according to those Scriptures, do You want me to know?"

_____

_____

_____

_____

Let yourself dream, and ask God: "How could believing these truths affect my life?"

_____

_____

_____

_____

Ask God: "What are some practical steps I can take to experience these truths in my life?"

_____

_____

_____

_____

_____

Now ask the Holy Spirit to empower you and make these truths more real in your life.

Identity

Take a moment to pray and reflect on these God-given aspects of your identity:

Filled with God's law

Given a new spirit

Given a heart of flesh

Walking in God's statutes

Obedient

Keeping God's rules

Clean from all uncleanness

Clean from all idols

Cleansed

Given a new heart

Perfected for all time

A letter of recommendation

A letter from Christ written with the Spirit of the living God

Sanctified

Write down a statement of faith of your own:

_____

_____

_____

_____

_____

_____

Additional thoughts for the day:

_____

_____

Day 18

Are You Chosen And Accepted?

You are held in great honor and worth in the sight of God. You are chosen and precious. Christ has received you, taken you to Himself, and granted you access to His heart as a friend. Therefore, receive one another as friends for the glory of God.

I appeal to you therefore, brothers, by the mercies of God, to present your bodies as a living sacrifice, holy and acceptable to God, which is your spiritual worship. Do not be conformed to this world, but be transformed by the renewal of your mind, that by testing you may discern what is the will of God, what is good and acceptable and perfect. *- Romans 12:1-2*

For the Kingdom of God is not a matter of eating and drinking but of righteousness and peace and joy in the Holy Spirit. Whoever thus serves Christ is acceptable to God and approved by men. So then let us pursue what makes for peace and for mutual upbuilding. *- Romans 14:17-19*

Therefore welcome one another as Christ has welcomed you, for the glory of God. *- Romans 15:7*

For we know, brothers loved by God, that He has chosen you, because our gospel came to you not only in word, but also in power and in the Holy Spirit and with full conviction. You know what kind of men we proved to be among you for your sake. *- 1 Thessalonians 1:4-5*

As you come to Him, a living stone rejected by men but in the sight of God chosen and precious, you yourselves like living stones are being built up as a spiritual house, to be a holy priesthood, to offer spiritual sacrifices acceptable to God through Jesus Christ. For it stands in Scripture: "Behold, I am laying in Zion a stone, a cornerstone chosen and precious, and whoever believes in Him will not be put to shame." *- 1 Peter 2:4-6*

But you are a chosen race, a royal priesthood, a holy nation, a people for His own possession, that you may proclaim the excellencies of Him who called you out of darkness into His marvelous light. Once you were not a people, but now you are God's people; once you had not received mercy, but now you have received mercy. *- 1 Peter 2:9-10*

Truth and Lies

Take a moment to pray and invite God to meet with you in this process. Reflect on the previous verses, and ask the Holy Spirit to reveal the truth of what God is saying in these Scriptures.

List the truth that was revealed to you:_____

_____

_____

_____

_____

Review the previous verses and ask the Lord to reveal any of your thoughts or feelings that may be opposed to the truth in those Scriptures.

Now ask the Lord what lies you believe that are connected to those thoughts and feelings.

List the lies that were revealed:_____

_____

_____

_____

Forgiveness and Repentance

As you review this list, ask the Lord if there is anyone you need to forgive that may have taught you, or hurt you with, these lies.

"In Jesus' name, I choose to forgive _____ for 'teaching me' or 'hurting me with' the lie that _____."

"In Jesus' name, I break agreement and renounce the lie that _____."

"Jesus, I come into agreement with Your forgiveness, and I completely forgive myself for any way I believed those lies. I release all those lies to You."

Statement of Faith

I am chosen by God and I am precious in His sight. I am a living sacrifice, holy and acceptable to God. I am able to discern and prove His will. Christ has welcomed me for the glory of God, and I will not be put to shame. My spiritual sacrifices are acceptable to God through Jesus. Like a living stone, I am being built up as a spiritual house to be a holy priest. God loves me and has chosen me to be a royal priest. He called me out of darkness and into His marvelous light. He called me to be His own, and to proclaim His greatness. God is great!

Now that you have forgiven, renounced the lies, and read the Statement of Faith, ask God: "What truths about my identity, according to those Scriptures, do You want me to know?"

_____

_____

_____

_____

_____

Let yourself dream, and ask God: "How could believing these truths affect my life?"

_____

_____

_____

_____

_____

Ask God: "What are some practical steps I can take to experience these truths in my life?"

_____

_____

_____

_____

_____

Now ask the Holy Spirit to empower you and make these truths more real in your life.

Identity

Take a moment to pray and reflect on these God-given aspects of your identity:

A brother/sister	Chosen	A royal priesthood
A living sacrifice	A living stone	A holy nation
Acceptable to God	A spiritual house	His own possession
Approved by men	A holy priesthood	Called into His marvelous light
Welcome	Not put to shame	
Loved by God	A chosen race	God's people

Write down a statement of faith of your own:

_____

_____

_____

_____

_____

_____

_____

Additional thoughts for the day:

_____

_____

_____

_____

_____

_____

_____

_____

Day 19

Are You Called And Do You Belong?

God, who is faithful, invited and called you by name into the fellowship of His Son, Jesus Christ our Lord. Therefore, you are encouraged to walk, live, and behave in a manner corresponding to, and properly fitting to, the worth of this personal invitation and calling by name. The Lord Himself has divinely called you.

...Jesus Christ our Lord, through whom we have received grace and apostleship to bring about the obedience of faith for the sake of His name among all the nations, including you who are called to belong to Jesus Christ. – *Romans 1:4b-6*

That by any means possible I may attain the resurrection from the dead. Not that I have already obtained this or am already perfect, but I press on to make it my own, because Christ Jesus has made me His own. – *Philippians 3:11-12*

I give thanks to my God always for you because of the grace of God that was given you in Christ Jesus, that in every way you were enriched in Him in all speech and all knowledge—even as the testimony about Christ was confirmed among you—so that you are not lacking in any gift, as you wait for the revealing of our Lord Jesus Christ, who will sustain you to the end, guiltless in the day of our Lord Jesus Christ. God is faithful, by whom you were called into the fellowship of His Son, Jesus Christ our Lord. – *1 Corinthians 1:4-9*

I do not cease to give thanks for you, remembering you in my prayers, that the God of our Lord Jesus Christ, the Father of glory, may give you the Spirit of wisdom and of revelation in the knowledge of Him, having the eyes of your hearts enlightened, that you may know what is the hope to which He has called you, what are the riches of His glorious inheritance in the saints, and what is the immeasurable greatness of His power toward us who believe, according to the working of His great might. – *Ephesians 1:16-19*

I therefore, a prisoner for the Lord, urge you to walk in a manner worthy of the calling to which you have been called, with all humility and gentleness, with patience, bearing with one another in love, eager to maintain the unity of the Spirit in the bond of peace. There is one body and one Spirit—just as you were called to the one hope that belongs to your call—one Lord, one faith, one baptism, one God and Father of all, who is over all and through all and in all. – *Ephesians 4:1-6*

Truth and Lies

Take a moment to pray and invite God to meet with you in this process. Reflect on the previous verses, and ask the Holy Spirit to reveal the truth of what God is saying in these Scriptures.

List the truth that was revealed to you:_____

_____

_____

_____

_____

Review the previous verses and ask the Lord to reveal any of your thoughts or feelings that may be opposed to the truth in those Scriptures.

Now ask the Lord what lies you believe that are connected to those thoughts and feelings.

List the lies that were revealed:_____

_____

_____

_____

_____

Forgiveness and Repentance

As you review this list, ask the Lord if there is anyone you need to forgive that may have taught you, or hurt you with, these lies.

"In Jesus' name, I choose to forgive _____ for 'teaching me' or 'hurting me with' the lie that _____."

"In Jesus' name, I break agreement and renounce the lie that _____."

"Jesus, I come into agreement with Your forgiveness, and I completely forgive myself for any way I believed those lies. I release all those lies to You."

Statement of Faith

God called me to belong to Jesus Christ. He has made me His own. The testimony of Christ is confirmed in me, and I am not lacking in any gift. In Jesus, I am enriched in all speech and knowledge. God has called me into the fellowship of His Son, and He will sustain me guiltless until the day of our Lord Jesus Christ. The Father of glory has given me the Spirit of wisdom and of revelation in the knowledge of Him. Having the eyes of my heart enlightened, I can know the hope to which He has called me. I can know the riches of His glorious inheritance in the saints.

Now that you have forgiven, renounced the lies, and read the Statement of Faith, ask God: "What truths about my identity, according to those Scriptures, do You want me to know?"

_____

_____

_____

_____

_____

Let yourself dream, and ask God: "How could believing these truths affect my life?"

_____

_____

_____

_____

_____

Ask God: "What are some practical steps I can take to experience these truths in my life?"

_____

_____

_____

_____

_____

Now ask the Holy Spirit to empower you and make these truths more real in your life.

Identity

Take a moment to pray and reflect on these God-given aspects of your identity:

Included

Called to belong to Jesus

His own

Given grace in Christ Jesus

Enriched in Him in all speech and all knowledge

Sustained guiltless

Called into the fellowship of His Son

Given the Spirit of wisdom and of revelation in the knowledge of Him

A saint

Humble

Gentle

Patient

Loving

Unified in the Spirit

Bonded in peace

Called to hope

Write down a statement of faith of your own:

_____

_____

_____

_____

_____

Additional thoughts for the day:

_____

_____

_____

_____

_____

_____

_____

_____

_____

Day 20

Are You Included And Sealed?

God, who establishes you in Christ, has anointed you and set His seal of security on you. He has proven you, marked you, and given you His Spirit in your heart as a guarantee. When you believed in Jesus Christ, you were authenticated and confirmed with the promised Holy Spirit, guaranteeing your inheritance.

In My Father's house are many rooms. If it were not so, would I have told you that I go to prepare a place for you? And if I go and prepare a place for you, I will come again and will take you to Myself, that where I am you may be also. *- John 14:2-3*

"The glory that you have given Me I have given to them, that they may be one even as We are one, I in them and You in Me, that they may become perfectly one, so that the world may know that You sent Me and loved them even as You loved Me. Father, I desire that they also, whom You have given Me, may be with Me where I am, to see My glory that You have given Me because You loved Me before the foundation of the world. O righteous Father, even though the world does not know You, I know You, and these know that You have sent Me. I made known to them Your name, and I will continue to make it known, that the love with which You have loved Me may be in them, and I in them." *- John 17:22-26*

In Him we have obtained an inheritance, having been predestined according to the purpose of Him who works all things according to the counsel of His will, so that we who were the first to hope in Christ might be to the praise of His glory. In Him you also, when you heard the word of truth, the gospel of your salvation, and believed in Him, were sealed with the promised Holy Spirit, who is the guarantee of our inheritance until we acquire possession of it, to the praise of His glory. *- Ephesians 1:11-14*

As surely as God is faithful, our word to you has not been Yes and No. For the Son of God, Jesus Christ, whom we proclaimed among you, Silvanus and Timothy and I, was not Yes and No, but in Him it is always Yes. For all the promises of God find their Yes in Him. That is why it is through Him that we utter our Amen to God for His glory. And it is God who establishes us with you in Christ, and has anointed us, and who has also put His seal on us and given us His Spirit in our hearts as a guarantee. *- 2 Corinthians 1:18-22*

Truth and Lies

Take a moment to pray and invite God to meet with you in this process. Reflect on the previous verses, and ask the Holy Spirit to reveal the truth of what God is saying in these Scriptures.

List the truth that was revealed to you:_____

_____

_____

_____

_____

Review the previous verses and ask the Lord to reveal any of your thoughts or feelings that may be opposed to the truth in those Scriptures.

Now ask the Lord what lies you believe that are connected to those thoughts and feelings.

List the lies that were revealed:_____

_____

_____

_____

Forgiveness and Repentance

As you review this list, ask the Lord if there is anyone you need to forgive that may have taught you, or hurt you with, these lies.

"In Jesus' name, I choose to forgive _____ for 'teaching me' or 'hurting me with' the lie that _____."

"In Jesus' name, I break agreement and renounce the lie that _____."

"Jesus, I come into agreement with Your forgiveness, and I completely forgive myself for any way I believed those lies. I release all those lies to You."

Statement of Faith

Jesus Himself is praying for me. He gave me His glory so that I may be one with Him, just as He is one with the Father. I am one with God. The Father loves me, even as He loves Jesus. Jesus desires for me to be with Him where He is. In Him, I have obtained an inheritance according to His purpose. I have been sealed with the promised Holy Spirit, guaranteeing my inheritance. I am established and anointed in Christ. My heart is filled with His Spirit.

Now that you have forgiven, renounced the lies, and read the Statement of Faith, ask God: "What truths about my identity, according to those Scriptures, do You want me to know?"

_____

_____

_____

_____

Let yourself dream, and ask God: "How could believing these truths affect my life?"

_____

_____

_____

_____

Ask God: "What are some practical steps I can take to experience these truths in my life?"

_____

_____

_____

_____

_____

Now ask the Holy Spirit to empower you and make these truths more real in your life.

Identity

Take a moment to pray and reflect on these God-given aspects of your identity:

Given glory

One with God

Perfectly one

Loved

Given to Jesus

With Jesus

An heir of His inheritance

Jesus in me

Predestined according to His purpose

Hopeful in Christ

The praise of His glory

Sealed with the promised Holy Spirit

Established in Christ

Anointed

Write down a statement of faith of your own:

_____

_____

_____

_____

_____

Additional thoughts for the day:

_____

_____

Day 21

Are You Approved And Blessed?

You have been proven, recognized as genuine, and deemed worthy to be entrusted with the gospel. Do your best to rightly handle the word of truth by presenting yourself to God as who you really are — a pleasing, valuable, approved, and acceptable worker, who has no need to be ashamed.

Now to the one who works, his wages are not counted as a gift but as his due. And to the one who does not work but believes in Him who justifies the ungodly, his faith is counted as righteousness, just as David also speaks of the blessing of the one to whom God counts righteousness apart from works: "Blessed are those whose lawless deeds are forgiven, and whose sins are covered; blessed is the man against whom the Lord will not count his sin." *– Romans 4:4-8*

Does He who supplies the Spirit to you and works miracles among you do so by works of the law, or by hearing with faith—just as Abraham "believed God, and it was counted to him as righteousness"? Know then that it is those of faith who are the sons of Abraham. And the Scripture, foreseeing that God would justify the Gentiles by faith, preached the gospel beforehand to Abraham, saying, "In you shall all the nations be blessed." So then, those who are of faith are blessed along with Abraham, the man of faith. *– Galatians 3:5-9*

Blessed be the God and Father of our Lord Jesus Christ, who has blessed us in Christ with every spiritual blessing in the heavenly places, even as He chose us in Him before the foundation of the world, that we should be holy and blameless before Him. In love He predestined us for adoption as sons through Jesus Christ, according to the purpose of His will, to the praise of His glorious grace, with which He has blessed us in the Beloved. In Him we have redemption through His blood, the forgiveness of our trespasses, according to the riches of His grace. *– Ephesians 1:3-7*

But just as we have been approved by God to be entrusted with the gospel, so we speak, not to please man, but to please God who tests our hearts. *– 1 Thessalonians 2:4*

Do your best to present yourself to God as one approved, a worker who has no need to be ashamed, rightly handling the word of truth. But avoid irreverent babble, for it will lead people into more and more ungodliness. *– 2 Timothy 2:15-16*

Truth and Lies

Take a moment to pray and invite God to meet with you in this process. Reflect on the previous verses, and ask the Holy Spirit to reveal the truth of what God is saying in these Scriptures.

List the truth that was revealed to you:_____

_____

_____

_____

_____

Review the previous verses and ask the Lord to reveal any of your thoughts or feelings that may be opposed to the truth in those Scriptures.

Now ask the Lord what lies you believe that are connected to those thoughts and feelings.

List the lies that were revealed:_____

_____

_____

_____

Forgiveness and Repentance

As you review this list, ask the Lord if there is anyone you need to forgive that may have taught you, or hurt you with, these lies.

"In Jesus' name, I choose to forgive _____ for 'teaching me' or 'hurting me with' the lie that _____."

"In Jesus' name, I break agreement and renounce the lie that _____."

"Jesus, I come into agreement with Your forgiveness, and I completely forgive myself for any way I believed those lies. I release all those lies to You."

Statement of Faith

I have been blessed and counted righteous, apart from my works. God has forgiven and covered my sins. He will never count them against me. I am blessed along with Abraham as a son/daughter. God, the Father of my Lord Jesus Christ, has blessed me with every spiritual blessing in the heavenly places. He has chosen me, in love, to be holy and blameless before Him as a son/daughter, through Jesus Christ. I am approved, blessed in the Beloved, and trusted with the good news of Jesus Christ. I am an approved worker and have no need to be ashamed.

Now that you have forgiven, renounced the lies, and read the Statement of Faith, ask God: "What truths about my identity, according to those Scriptures, do You want me to know?"

_____

_____

_____

_____

_____

Let yourself dream, and ask God: "How could believing these truths affect my life?"

_____

_____

_____

_____

_____

Ask God: "What are some practical steps I can take to experience these truths in my life?"

_____

_____

_____

_____

_____

Now ask the Holy Spirit to empower you and make these truths more real in your life.

Identity

Take a moment to pray and reflect on these God-given aspects of your identity:

Counted righteous apart from my works

Blessed

Forgiven

Covered

A son/daughter of Abraham

Blessed along with Abraham

Holy and blameless before Him

Chosen in Him

Blessed in Christ with every spiritual blessing in the heavenly places

Predestined for adoption as a son/daughter through Jesus Christ

Blessed in the Beloved

Redeemed through His blood

Forgiven according to the riches of His grace

Approved by God

Entrusted with the gospel

Approved

A worker who has no need to be ashamed

Write down a statement of faith of your own:

_____

_____

_____

_____

_____

_____

Additional thoughts for the day:

_____

_____

_____

_____

_____

_____

_____

_____

_____

APPENDIX

Statements of Faith

Day 1

I have redemption in Jesus through His blood. My sins have been forgiven according to the riches of His grace. God lavished all this upon me, in all wisdom and insight, making known to me the mystery of His will, according to His purpose, which He set forth in Christ. Christ redeemed me from the curse of the law by becoming a curse for me. In Christ Jesus, the blessing of Abraham came to me, so that I could receive the promised Spirit through faith. Jesus is the mediator of a new covenant for me. He called me and gave me the promised eternal inheritance. Jesus gave Himself for me to redeem me from all lawlessness and to purify me for Himself.

Day 2

God demonstrates His righteousness by being my justifier. I have been justified freely by God's grace, through the redemption that is in Christ Jesus. Therefore, since I am justified by faith, I have peace with God through our Lord Jesus Christ. I am an heir according to the hope of eternal life by the blood of Jesus.

Day 3

I have been sanctified in the truth; Your Word is truth. God Himself, the God of peace, sanctifies me completely. He has perfected me for all time, through the single offering of Jesus Christ.

Day 4

I am saved by grace and made alive together with Christ. God has raised me up with Christ and seated me with Him in heavenly places. Through the blood of Jesus Christ, He brought me near to Himself. I have been set free from sin and have become a slave to righteousness. For freedom, Christ has set me free. I am clean because of the word Jesus spoke over me. He reconciled me through His body, and now presents me holy, blameless, and free from accusation. I am a new creation in Christ. The old is gone and the new has come. All this is from God, who reconciled me to Himself, and made me a member of His household. God created me in Christ Jesus for good works.

Day 5

My old self has been crucified with Christ. When I was still just a sinner, Jesus condemned sin in my flesh so that my old body of sin was brought to nothing. I was united with Him in His death and buried with Him in baptism. I am dead to sin, no longer a slave to sin, and I have been set free from sin in Christ Jesus.

Day 6

By grace, I am united with Christ in His resurrection. It is no longer my old self who lives, but Christ who lives in me. By faith, I am made righteous through Jesus, and I reign with Him in newness of life. The old has passed away and the new has come. I am saved by grace, and grace reigns through me for eternal life. I am a new creation in Christ. I am alive in the Spirit and I live to God.

Day 7

I am set free in Christ, and my life is hidden with Him in God. I am not in the flesh, I am not controlled by the flesh, and I do not live according to the flesh. I am in the Spirit and live according to the Spirit. The Spirit dwells in me and gives me life. I am alive to God and I belong to Christ Jesus. He lives in me, and I have life and peace because my mind is set on the things of the Spirit.

Day 8

I have been brought from death to life. All of me is new. I have been created after the likeness of God as an instrument of true righteousness and holiness. I am an approved, holy, and acceptable living sacrifice, being renewed in the knowledge of my Creator. I can discern the will of God – what is His good, acceptable, and perfect will.

Day 9

By faith, as an offspring of Abraham, I am guaranteed to be an heir of the promise. I am in Christ. God is my wisdom, righteousness, sanctification, and redemption. I have become the righteousness of God in Jesus Christ. I am blessed. My sins are forgiven, covered, and will never be counted against me.

Day 10

I am in Christ and set free from condemnation. God sent His own Son, in the likeness of sinful flesh, to condemn sin in my flesh. The righteous requirements of the law are fulfilled in me. I walk according to the Spirit, with my mind set on the things of the Spirit. I am in the Spirit, and my mind is filled with life and peace. The Spirit dwells in me, and my spirit is alive because of righteousness.

Day 11

I am fearfully and wonderfully made in God's image. Before I was even born, God prepared good works for me to walk in. He will bring these to completion. I am a partner with Him in the gospel of grace. I am filled with the fruit of righteousness through Jesus.

Day 12

All grace abounds to me. I have all sufficiency, in all things, at all times, to abound in every good work. I am filled with the knowledge of His will, with all spiritual wisdom and understanding, so that I can walk in a manner worthy of the Lord. I am fully pleasing to Him, bearing fruit in every good work. I am strengthened with all power according to His glorious might. He made me worthy *of His calling, and I am qualified and equipped with everything good. God is fulfilling His will in me. He is doing the work He prepared for me, for His good pleasure. Jesus is glorified in me, and I am glorified in Jesus. God loves me and eternally comforts me with hope through grace.*

Day 13

My flesh, with its passions and desires, has been crucified. I live in Christ. My life in Christ is a life of fruitful labor. My fruitful labor is faith working through love. I walk in the Spirit and I am led by the Spirit. I am a child of light: a good, right, and true light in this world. I live by the Spirit and keep in step with the Spirit. The grace of God is training me to renounce all ungodliness, and live an upright, godly life. Jesus purified me as His own and made me zealous for good works.

Day 14

I am God's beloved, purified possession. Jesus gave Himself for me so that I could be spotless, without blemish, and free from accusation. He washed me clean, and sanctified me by the word that He spoke to me and over me. He chose me, in Him, to be holy and blameless. I am holy and blameless. I am a dearly loved saint: a guiltless, faultless, clean, and pure saint.

Day 15

I was called into fellowship with Jesus. I abound in love, with more and more knowledge and discernment. I am pure, blameless, and filled with the fruit of righteousness. He is completing the good work He started in me, and will sustain me guiltless until the end. The Lord increases my love for all the saints. My heart is established as blameless and holy before God, with all the saints. The God of peace is faithful; He is sanctifying me completely. God is able to keep me from stumbling, and present my whole spirit, soul, and body blameless in His presence.

Day 16

Jesus has purified my conscience from dead works, and has secured an eternal redemption for me. He mediated a new covenant so that I could receive His promised, eternal inheritance. By the will of God, Jesus' single offering has redeemed me, sanctified me, and perfected me for all time. He appeared on my behalf. God will never again remember my sins and lawless deeds. Jesus has washed my heart and my body clean. He wants me to draw near to Him, with my heart full of the assurance of His faithful promises. God's Word is written on my pure heart and my clean mind. I have confidence to enter the holy places by the blood of Jesus.

Day 17

God is my God, and I belong to Him. He has cleansed me and removed all my false idols. By Jesus' single offering, He has forgiven all of my sins and will remember them no more. He has removed my old heart of stone, and given me a new heart of flesh. He has written His laws on my mind and my heart. Jesus has given me a new spirit and has perfected me for all time. His Holy Spirit empowers me to walk in His statutes. I am a letter from Christ, written with the Spirit of the living God, on the tablet of my heart.

Day 18

I am chosen by God and I am precious in His sight. I am a living sacrifice, holy and acceptable to God. I am able to discern and prove His will. Christ has welcomed me for the glory of God, and I will not be put to shame. My spiritual sacrifices are acceptable to God through Jesus. Like a living stone, I am being built up as a spiritual house to be a holy priest. God loves me and has chosen me to be a royal priest. He called me out of darkness and into His marvelous light. He called me to be His own, and to proclaim His greatness. God is great!

Day 19

God called me to belong to Jesus Christ. He has made me His own. The testimony of Christ is confirmed in me, and I am not lacking in any gift. In Jesus, I am enriched in all speech and knowledge. God has called me into the fellowship of His Son, and He will sustain me guiltless until the day of our Lord Jesus Christ. The Father of glory has given me the Spirit of wisdom and of revelation in the knowledge of Him. Having the eyes of my heart enlightened, I can know the hope to which He has called me. I can know the riches of His glorious inheritance in the saints.

Day 20

Jesus Himself is praying for me. He gave me His glory so that I may be one with Him, just as He is one with the Father. I am one with God. The Father loves me, even as He loves Jesus. Jesus desires for me to be with Him where He is. In Him, I have obtained an inheritance according to His purpose. I have been sealed with the promised Holy Spirit, guaranteeing my inheritance. I am established and anointed in Christ. My heart is filled with His Spirit.

Day 21

I have been blessed and counted righteous, apart from my works. God has forgiven and covered my sins. He will never count them against me. I am blessed along with Abraham as a son/daughter. God, the Father of my Lord Jesus Christ, has blessed me with every spiritual blessing in the heavenly places. He has chosen me, in love, to be holy and blameless before Him as a son/daughter, through Jesus Christ. I am approved, blessed in the Beloved, and trusted with the good news of Jesus Christ. I am an approved worker and have no need to be ashamed.

Identity

A brother/sister

A child of God

A child of light

A chosen race

A fellow citizen

A fellow heir with Christ

A guaranteed heir of the promise

A holy nation

A holy priesthood

A letter from Christ written with the Spirit of the living God

A letter of recommendation

A living sacrifice

A living stone

A member of God's household

A minister of reconciliation

A new creation

A partaker of grace

A partner in the gospel

A royal priesthood

A saint

A servant of the living God

A slave of righteousness

A slave to God

A son/daughter of Abraham

A spiritual house

A worker who has no need to be ashamed

Able to discern the will of God

Abounding in every good work

Abounding in love

Above reproach

Above reproach before Him

Abraham's offspring

Acceptable to God

Adopted as a son/daughter

Alive

Alive to God

Alive together with Christ

An approved worker

An heir according to the hope of eternal life

An heir of God

An heir of His inheritance

An instrument for righteousness

Anointed

Approved

Approved by God

Approved by men

At peace with God

Baptized into Christ Jesus

Bearing fruit in every good work

Belonging to Christ Jesus

Belonging to Him

Beloved

Blameless

Blessed

Blessed along with Abraham

Blessed in Christ

Blessed in Christ with every spiritual blessing in the heavenly places

Blessed in the Beloved

Bonded in peace

Brought from death to life

Brought near

Called

Called into His marvelous light

Called into the fellowship of His Son

Called to belong to Jesus

Called to hope

Chosen

Chosen in Him

Christ in me

Clean

Clean from all idols

Clean from all uncleanness

Clean hearted

Cleansed

Confident to enter the holy places

Counted righteous apart from my works

Covered

Created after the likeness of God

Created in Christ Jesus for good works

Created in true righteousness and true holiness

Crucified with Christ

Dead to sin

Eagerly waiting for Him

Enriched in Him

Enriched in Him in all speech and all knowledge

Entrusted with the gospel

Equipped with everything good

Established in Christ

Established in every good work and word

Established in holiness before God

Eternally alive in Christ Jesus

Eternally redeemed

Faithful

Fearfully and wonderfully made

Filled with God's law

Filled with the fruit of
righteousness

Filled with the knowledge of His
will

Filled with the righteous
requirements of the law

Filled with the Spirit

Forgiven

Forgiven according to the riches
of His grace

Formed by God

Free

Free from the law of sin and
death

Fruitful

Fully assured in faith

Fully pleasing to Him

Gentle

Given a heart of flesh

Given a new heart

Given a new spirit

Given glory

Given grace in Christ Jesus

Given the Spirit of wisdom and
of revelation in the knowledge
of Him

Given to Jesus

Glorified with Him

God's people

Godly in this present age

Good

Having all sufficiency in all
things at all times

Hidden with Christ in God

His own

His own possession

His possession

His saint

His workmanship

Holy

Holy and blameless before Him

Hopeful in Christ

Humble

In Christ

In Christ Jesus

In glory

In the Spirit

Included

Increasing and abounding in
love

Increasing in the knowledge of God

Indwelled with the Spirit

Jesus in me

Joyful

Justified

Justified by faith

Justified by His blood

Justified by His grace

Keeping God's rules

Keeping in step with the Spirit

Kept blameless

Kept from stumbling

Kind

Led by the Spirit

Light in the Lord

Living according to the Spirit

Living by the Spirit

Living to God

Loved

Loved by God

Loving

New

No longer enslaved to sin

Not condemned

Not in the flesh

Not lacking in any gift

Not of the world

Not put to shame

Not under the law

Obedient

Obedient from the heart

One with God

Patient

Peaceful

Perfected for all time

Perfectly one

Pleasing in His sight

Predestined according to His purpose

Predestined for adoption as a son/daughter through Jesus Christ

Presented blameless

Presented in splendor

Promised an eternal inheritance

Promised the Holy Spirit

Pure

Pure and blameless for the day of Christ

Pure in conscience

Purified for Him

Purified from dead works

Purified from dead works to serve the living God

Qualified to share in the inheritance of the saints in light

Raised up with Him

Raised with Christ

Reconciled in His body

Reconciled to Him

Redeemed

Redeemed from all lawlessness

Redeemed from the curse

Redeemed in Christ Jesus

Redeemed through His blood

Regenerated

Rejoicing in hope

Renewed

Renewed in knowledge after the image of my Creator

Right

Righteous

Righteous apart from works

Sanctified

Sanctified completely

Sanctified in truth

Sanctified through the offering of Jesus Christ

Saved

Saved according to His own mercy

Saved by Him

Saved by His life

Sealed with the promised Holy Spirit

Seated with Him

Seated with Him in the heavenly places

Secure in an eternal redemption

Self-controlled

Sent by Jesus

Set free

Set free from sin

Set free in Christ

Set on the things of the Spirit

Spiritually wise and understanding

Standing in grace

Strengthened with all power

Sustained guiltless

Sustained guiltless to the end

The praise of His glory

The righteousness of God

Trained to renounce ungodliness

True

True hearted

Unashamed

Unified in the Spirit

United in Him

United with Him

United with Him in resurrection

Upright

Walking according to the Spirit

Walking in God's statutes

Walking in newness of life

Washed

Washed with pure water

Welcome

With Jesus

Without blemish

Without spot or wrinkle

Working for His good pleasure

Worthy of His calling

Worthy of the Lord

Zealous for good works